I want to commend Ken Roberts—primarily, for his wisdom and sensitivity to this present hour, as the increasing pressure and disorientation of focus many pastors and other leaders face today. *Staying Power* is written by a good shepherd—a man who understands the dynamics of seeking to remember one's initial vision and to retain our sense of mission amid the flurry of testings, trials and just plain tiredness that so easily deter sincere people who *do care*, but also *need care*.

With discernment, humility and unpretentious self-disclosure, you'll find Ken readily identify with each one of us who seek to serve Christ with integrity and devotion. While maintaining ideals, the hard realities that strain their maintenance are faced, presenting us with a very practical book. I rejoice in its availability, believing it will bless, build-up and embolden with encouragement many; strengthening each one who, like me, needs solid, spiritually founded assistance and guidelines for our journey, irrespective of our calling.

Pastor Jack Hayford
Chancellor, The King's University, Dallas – Los Angeles

Ken Roberts' *Staying Power: 5 Core Ideas to Sustainability in Christian Leadership* is an important book for pastors and seminarians. It is an anti-quantitative church growth book and a pro-qualitative growth resource—written for the inner health and wholeness of both the pastor and the congregation. Echoing insights from his mentor Dallas Willard, Ken Roberts offers a clear call for unhurried being over performance-driven doing.

Gary W. Moon, M.Div., PhD
Executive Director Dallas Willard
Author, *Apprenticeship with Jesus*

D1637216

I spend a lot of time ministering to hurting and frustrated church leaders. They are everywhere. That's why this book is so important. It is filled with relevant, compassionate, insightful wisdom. If you are a pastor, you owe it to yourself to read Ken's book.

Richard Blackaby, PhD
Co-author of *Experiencing God, Spiritual Leadership*

With all the talk these days about ministerial burnout and the discouraging statistics about dropout, Ken Roberts brings a much needed encouraging word about sustainability in ministry and God's provision to provide the strength for a long-term, healthy ministry. Do ministers face problems? Yes. But there is an answer! Thanks Ken for a much needed reminder that ministry and health actually go together.

Gordon Anderson, Ph.D.
President, North Central University, Minneapolis, Minnesota

Ken Roberts has successfully combined the rawness of life experience with great reflective thought in this very readable volume. I was immediately drawn into the book by the fluency of the text and Ken's keen insights. Ken displays the rare gift of combining emotion, reflection and good theological thought in this book. As a result I heartily recommend it and believe that it will take its rightful place within the genre of narrative theology.

Paul R Alexander, PhD
President, Trinity Bible College, Ellendale, ND
Chair, World Alliance for Pentecostal Theological Education

Staying Power is engaging, contemplative, and real. Ken's self-awareness and ability to unveil personal foibles and failures are relatable and transferrable for every Christian minister. Get ready to embrace and implement change toward more viable and enjoyable sustainability!

Jim Palmer
Assistant Superintendent of the Assemblies of God,
Ohio District

We spend a lot of time and energy discussing effectiveness and efficiency. We need to add sustainability to the list. Leaders who live and lead well for decades are extraordinarily rare. My friend, Ken Roberts, is one of those leaders. He has pondered, prayed about, and poked around the idea of how leaders can develop "staying power." This book is the result of that quest. You become a seasoned leader by navigating different seasons, some fun and exciting and some tragic and unbearable. Ken has done all of the above and is still standing, leaning forward and living a life of intimacy and impact. In this book he will help you do the same thing.

Chip Judd
Pastor, Counselor, Speaker, Seacoast Church Charlotte S.C.

Since I've known the author for 30 years, my endorsement is biased. But this also enables me to commend him and his book as a masterful work of authenticity and practicality. If you're like me and want to continue learning and improving, this book is for you!

Larry Tomczak
Best-selling author and cultural commentator

In my travels around the world, ministering to Pastors and ministry leaders, I hear what I call the "silent cry." From Eastern Europe to South Africa, Central America to Asia, and of course right here in the USA, I hear this quiet plea. Leaders are looking for someone to introduce answers to the internal challenges that many ministers simply aren't dealing with. Not because they don't want to. They just don't know how.

I am personally grateful for the time, energy, commitment, passion, and raw heart that Ken has placed at the doorsteps of our lives and ministries. If you have ever wished that someone would "rescue" you from this seemingly ambiguous ministry world, you need to read this book.

Ed Huie
Founder and President, Echo Ministries

Ken Roberts, in this work addresses a critical need in today's church – the casualty rate among Christian leaders. Scripture, as well as church history, give evidence that not all who are called by God prove faithful to their calling. However, the premise of this book is that the state of Christian leadership in the church is at an *all-time crisis*. Ken does not simply present the problem; he provides logical and Scriptural answers to this current dilemma.

Harold Helms, Th.D, D.D.
Pastor for 50 years

What Ken Roberts has done in the book, *Staying Power: 5 Core Ideas To Sustainability in Christian Leadership,* is remarkable. His honest approach to his own pain draws a reader in and opens the door for the reader to be vulnerable about his or her own struggles. The book can help a leader lead in a way that is honest, and sustainable. These stories will inspire you to tell your own, and then your story will inspire others to tell their story.

Daniel K Mundt
Heartland Supervisor for the Foursquare Church

Pastor Ken's ability to communicate complex ideas around leadership in tangible, easy to digest ways is remarkable. He writes as he lives — a constant source of wise counsel for young pastors. As a church planter his teaching on leading from the inside out and focus on spiritual growth has been right on the money. Whether you have been in ministry for decades or are a young pastor like me, I can't think of another leader I would more highly recommend.

Geoff Bullock
Church Planter

As a professor, pastor and mom I know how easy it is to get pulled in many different directions and put my own spiritual growth on the back burner. Pastor Ken is a master communicator who writes from decades as a pastor and leader who truly gets what it means to lead from a place of integrity and personal spiritual growth. I often say that God is more concerned about what's happening in us, than what is happening through us. If you are interested in growing spiritually as you lead then I recommend you read Ken's book.

Nicole Bullock
Professor, Mom, Church Planter

STAYING POWER

5 CORE IDEAS TO SUSTAINABILITY IN CHRISTIAN LEADERSHIP

KEN L ROBERTS

A Live Better, Lead Better Resource

A Live Better, Lead Better Resource
Maple Grove, MN. 55311
www.kenlroberts.com

ISBN 978-0-9861378-0-8

ISBN 978-0-9861378-1-5 (for ebook)

Library of Congress Cataloging-in-Publication Data

A Live Better, Lead Better Resource
18901 97th Place N
Maple Grove, MN 55311
www.kenlroberts.com

Cover Design By:
Ben Spinler
www.7rendered.com

Interior Design By:
Jeffrey Jansen
aestheticsoup.net

Live better. Lead better.

DEDICATION

To three of the most influential men in my life

Pastor Jack Hayford

The late Dallas Willard

And

My father, Reverend James E. Roberts

CONTENTS

CONSIDERING THE PROBLEM

5 CORE IDEAS TO SUSTAINABILITY

A FINAL CHALLENGE

CHAPTER ONE

TRUE CONFESSIONS OF TODAY'S CHRISTIAN LEADERS

Houston, we have a problem.

APOLLO 13

I awoke knowing my life was about to change.

In my dream, I sat in the large sanctuary of a well-known Christian leader. Although I had only met this pastor once, and it was a brief encounter, I actually knew him quite well. I had read his books, listened to his teaching tapes, tuned into his weekly radio broadcast, and watched him on Christian TV. He wasn't aware of it, but he had been a mentor to me since my early days as a student in seminary. In fact, he had been so influential in my life that for the past twenty-five years, I had modeled much of my own ministry after his.

I had never been in the sanctuary of his church, but instinctively I knew this was where my dream had carried me. I was sitting half way down on the right side of the packed auditorium waiting for the service to begin, when my mentor walked across the platform, opened a black leather binder, and placed it on the podium. He straightened his back, squared his shoulders, and took a deep breath. Before he said a word, I sensed what was about to happen, and I began to weep. He read a few words from his notes and was overcome with emotion. Cradling his face in his hands, he slowly lowered his head to the podium. He too began to weep. After a few moments, through his tears, he shared with the congregation that he deeply loved and had faithfully served for more than thirty years, his decision to resign.

I awoke from the dream and immediately understood its implications.

The last four years of my life as a pastor had been hellish, a stark contrast to the many years I had previously experienced. From its inception, the church I pastored had possessed a golden touch. Within a few short years, we had grown to one of the largest charismatic churches in our city. We were known for the passion of our worship, the excellence of our performing arts, and the overall vitality of our spiritual community. We were respected and trusted among both charismatic and evangelical churches in our area. As a result, we had helped initiate and support several Christian endeavors within our city, our region, and around the world.

But that once golden touch had waned, and the last four years felt as if we were making bricks without straw. Everything was hard. We experienced one grinding season after another. We would gear up to take one step forward only to take two steps back. One disappointment would be followed by yet another. Perseverance became our daily motto and survival became our main mission.

First, we experienced a difficult and depleting building project. Similar to a stormy marriage engagement, our plans were on, then off, then on, then off again. After ten years of starts and stops, the 42-acre campus, 55,000 square foot building, and 1300 seat state of the art auditorium – with a ten million dollar price tag – was finally complete. But not without it first taking a titanic toll on all of us. With more than a million dollars in cost overruns and a sudden down turn in the economy, when we moved into our new facility and didn't experience the expected and needed growth, the financial pressures became enormous. *(I learned the hard way that what Kevin Costner said in the movie Field of Dreams, "if you build it [they] will come" isn't always true.)* The dream of having our own facility quickly became a nightmare and the previous hassles of setting up and tearing down in a high school auditorium every Sunday – for over twenty years – didn't seem like such a headache anymore.

Then, after only nine months in our new building, we experienced a trauma from which we never fully recovered. On a routine drive to a women's bible study, my wife of twenty-five years was killed in a car accident. Like a direct torpedo hit into the side of an already beleaguered battle ship, it was a devastating blow. Our church weathered it for a while but the tragedy eventually crippled us.

The final blow was the unraveling of our pastoral team, most of whom had served together for almost twenty years.

The financial pressures of our new building and the shattering impact of the loss of my wife widened the divisions already among us. Like a broken windshield, the cracks quickly spread throughout our entire congregation. The erosion brought about through ongoing misunderstandings, unresolved conflicts, and blatant mistrust, picked up speed. Like a mud slide, everything began to give way. One by one, members of our pastoral team began disbanding and drifting away – some to saner and safer places, and others, not sure where to go, just anywhere but here. Cherished friendships were broken, and our once compelling dream crumbled. Wounded and disillusioned, many members within our congregation also began walking away.

During this season, I too wondered whether I should resign from the church I deeply loved and walk away. My journal entry on the morning of my 50th birthday describes my struggle with this difficult decision.

> I'm uncertain of my future role as the Senior Pastor of Worldview Community Church. I'm not only uncertain of my role, I'm uncertain of our church's very survival. We are really struggling right now. And even if our church does survive, I'm not sure I want to, or should, continue as her pastor.
>
> I'm not even sure I want to remain in the ministry. If I'm completely honest and true to my deepest longings, if I had some extra money or knew how to make a decent living doing something else – anything else – I would leave pastoring altogether. At times, I just want to get out of the

battle zone and live my own life! I've felt this very, very strong lately. This coming year may determine the future direction of my life and ministry.

(November 27th, 2006)

I wasn't naïve. I knew a lot was at stake with my decision.

From a professional perspective, my entire life as a pastor had been identified with this one church. I had worked extremely hard, and fought many battles to establish a church of significant size and substantial influence. In this city where I pastored, I had developed deep and meaningful friendships with many of my colleagues. I had always believed that it was in this *one* church, in this *one* city, where God had placed me and promised me a fulfilling and fruitful inheritance, ever since I had moved to this city twenty-two years earlier. So what did all of this mean to me now?

On a more personal note, this was the only church my two children (now grown) had ever known. And, without question the most agonizing part of the decision was that I had buried my beloved wife in a cemetery plot on a hill overlooking our church campus. Could I walk away from all of this? Should I walk away from it?

But like a pregnancy come full term, almost nine months to the day that I had the dream about my mentor, I walked across the stage of our auditorium, stepped to the podium, opened my notes and resigned as the Senior Pastor of the congregation I deeply loved and had faithfully served for over twenty-five years.

And like my mentor, I too wept.

MORE TRUE CONFESSIONS

Your experience in Christian ministry may or may not be as turbulent or tragic as mine. But, if you've led for any length of time, you too have dealt with the difficult days of leading. Whether these days were brought about by a barrage of accusations, the sting of betrayal, a congregational coup, or the consequences of your own doing – we've all encountered the challenges involved in leading. These difficult days of leadership have plunged some leaders into heavy discouragement or deep depression. Others have been pushed into emotional or physical breakdown. Then there are those who have been so devastated and disillusioned by their experiences in Christian leadership, they've outright abandoned their faith. Wherever you fall on this spectrum, all of us at one time or another, have felt the overwhelming temptation to turn and walk away.

Wayne Coerderio did.

In his book, *Leading on Empty*, this internationally known Christian leader, records his own story of burnout and breakdown. Pastor Coerderio writes:

> For over thirty years my drive for excellence propelled me. It wasn't that I was compulsive; I simply had a deep desire to do my best. I drove hard on all cylinders, not realizing that being an entrepreneur means that everything you initiate, by default you must add to your maintenance list.
>
> I pioneered a church, so I became its senior pastor. Starting several other churches made me the director of church planting. We went on to plant over a hundred

churches, and the unspoken expectation is that when you have children, you take care of them. And you know how that goes. When the children go astray, the missing-child report indicts you as the bad parent. In addition, my desire to train emerging leaders found me the president of our newly formed Pacific Rim Bible College.

Mind you, I loved every bit of what I was doing, but all too soon I had a tiger by the tail, and I couldn't let go. It is a gift to be able to launch an inspiring vision. But unless you manage it along the way, it can turn on you, and soon the voracious appetite of the vision consumes you.

Our congregation grew to over fourteen thousand in twelve years with nine campuses linked by video downloads. I had authored eight books. The *Life Journal* I had developed required a shipping department in order to service the wonderful churches who were partnering with us.

Now I found myself managing more than leading and dropping as many plates as I was spinning.

Then my father passed away, and within a span of two years my wife lost both of her parents. We had some struggles with our youngest, and a dear friend with whom I had begun the ministry moved on to other things. I felt like I was being swept along in a swift-moving current. My only hope was that the current would be merciful enough to push me to the side of the bank before I was dragged into the undertow of the rapids.

Finally it came to a head while I was out on a run on that balmy California evening. One minute I was jogging along on the sidewalk, and the next minute I was sitting on the curb, sobbing uncontrollably. I couldn't stop, and I didn't have a clue what was happening to me. [1]

Doug Bannister, at one time the pastor of one of America's fastest growing churches, makes his own confession concerning the darker side of Christian leadership. In his book *Sacred Quest* he writes:

The trappings of evangelical success soon began to come my way – we were honored as one of America's fastest growing churches and cited in church growth books. Articles on our church's ministries appeared frequently in our denominational magazine. When the presidency of our denomination came open, I was invited to apply. Attendance continued to rise.

I began to receive numerous requests to speak from around the country and overseas. Many of the life goals I had set when I was in college were being filled. I completed my doctorate and published my first book… We built another, much larger, worship center to accommodate the swelling crowds, and planted our first daughter church. As my thirties drew to a close, it appeared I could say with David, 'The boundary lines have fallen for me in pleasant places; surely I have a delightful inheritance.'

Appearances, however, are deceiving. What I had inherited as my ministry continued to expand was anything but delightful. I had inherited *a broken inner world.* Even as my pastoral "career" was scoring high marks, *my inner world was slowly unraveling.* [2]

From my own story, to the confessions of these two high profile leaders, as well as stories from many of my colleagues – the same confessions continue to surface among today's Christian leaders. Whether from large or small, urban or suburban, Catholic or charismatic, the countless and candid conversations convened behind closed doors only confirm the fact that the condition of today's Christian leaders has crested to a state of crisis. Like a tsunami arriving on our shore, none of us are spared from its impact.

SOME DISTURBING STATS

It's not only these confessions that convince us of our current condition, but the statistics also confirm this crisis. Below is a summary of different statistics from different sources about the state of today's Christian leadership. They are disturbing.

- 45 percent of pastors' wives say the greatest danger to them and their family is physical, emotional, mental, and spiritual burnout.
- 52 percent of pastors say they and their spouses believe that being in pastoral ministry is hazardous to their family's well-being and health.
- 75 percent report that they've had a significant

stress-related crisis at least once in their ministry.

- Clergy have the second highest divorce rate among all professions.
- 80 percent of adult children of pastors surveyed have had to seek professional help for depression.
- 90 percent of pastors work 55 to 75 hours a week.
- 80 percent of pastors say they have insufficient time with their spouse.
- 25 percent of pastors' wives see their husband's work schedule as a source of conflict.
- 56 percent of pastors' wives say they have no close friends.
- 70 percent of pastors say they do not have someone they consider a close friend.
- 45.5 percent of pastors say they've experienced depression or burnout to the extent that they need to take a leave of absence from ministry.
- 70 percent have a lower self-image now than when they started in the ministry.
- 80 percent of pastors and 84 percent of their spouses feel unqualified and discouraged in their role as pastors.
- 50 percent are so discouraged that they would leave the ministry if they could, but they have no other way of making a living.
- 50 percent have considered leaving the ministry in the last month.
- 50 percent of those who start out in ministry will not last 5 years.

- 80 percent of seminary and Bible school graduates who enter the ministry will leave the ministry within 5 years.
- Only 1 out of 10 ministers will actually retire as a minister in some form. [3 & 4]

As these statistics show, and many of the stories from today's Christian leaders further confirm, "Houston we have a problem!"

I don't want to suggest I'm speaking for the current state of *all* Christian leaders. That would be inaccurate and arrogant. Nor do I want to over generalize, over simplify, or over dramatize the issue. That wouldn't be helpful either. There are thousands of godly and gifted, compassionate and committed, skillful and sacrificial, men and women all across our nation and around our world, who faithfully serve Christ and His Church. So I don't want to overstate the problem.

If you're a leader who's dealing with discouragement or depression, I don't want to weigh you down with more bad news. We've had enough stones thrown our way; we certainly don't need more self-righteous critics. I don't want to be one.

If you're a leader who's experienced the shame of a moral failure, or you're someone struggling with ongoing and unwanted areas of compromise, I'm not here to waggle a finger in your face. Being involved in leadership is difficult enough, and I certainly don't want to add more injury to our already beleaguered and battered "profession." I'm sincerely writing as a fellow traveler with my own war wounds and spiritual wanderings, who deeply loves God's church and truly honors His leaders.

PURPOSE AND STRUCTURE

What I do hope to accomplish in *Staying Power* is simple and straightforward. I want to initiate a conversation around some central questions:

As a Christian leader, is there a way to do life and leadership in which over time we become healthier and more holistic, not less?

As a Christian leader, are there some foundational ideas that can help us build a life of sustainability in Christian leadership?

Raising awareness to the current crisis among Christian leaders, and offering a framework to discuss some of these critical questions is crucial – and urgent. The sooner we get honest with the problem, the sooner a healthy dialogue can occur, and movement toward a healthier and more holistic Christian leadership community can emerge.

I want to approach this topic from a slightly different angle than what might be expected or what's been offered in other books. Granted, there are some key practices to building a life of sustainability in Christian leadership. Personal devotions, keeping a clear conscience, building a strong marriage and family, managing stress, balancing home and work, good time management, exercising and eating right, building a support network, and other such practices are all important to building a life of sustainability in Christian leadership.

In *Staying Power*, I want to look at some of the deeper root issues that I believe are the primary reasons for the condition of many of today's Christian leaders. To do so I've structured the book around three categories:

• Presenting the Problem – chapters one through five

- Offering 5 Core Ideas To Sustainability – chapters six through eleven
- Concluding with a Final Challenge – chapter twelve

HOW TO USE THIS BOOK
- *Action and Application:*

At the end of each chapter I've included a one page Action and Application section. The page offers reflection questions and recommended actions. Since I was not able to be exhaustive on the topics covered in each chapter, I've also added in this same section some recommended resources. These are some of the best books I've read on the topic of that particular chapter. They can be referenced for deeper study if you so desire.

- *Group Study:*

Staying Power is also highly recommended for group study. The book is ideal for church staffs, boards, leadership teams, ministry teams, and aspiring leaders. Even though the book is written more specifically for Christian leaders, I highly recommend it to every person who loves God's church and God's leaders within His church. This is a problem we all need to be aware of, and something all of us can make a positive contribution toward.

DREAM WITH ME
Near the end of my four hellish years of leadership, I sat overlooking Lake Erie on a beautiful August day. Once again I began to weep. This time I wasn't weeping because of a dream I'd had, or because of my own resignation as a senior pastor.

This time I wept for a different reason. It was because of a new dream that was starting to stir deep in my soul.

As I sat there on that August afternoon, here are the words that stirred my soul and caused me to weep.

> When we are in touch with our *deepest longings* a whole different set of choices open up. Rather than being motivated by guilt and obligation we are compelled to seek out ways of living *that are congruent with our deepest desires.* Sometimes this feels risky, and it often opens up a whole new set of questions, but this is fundamentally what spiritual transformation is all about: choosing a way of life that opens us to the presence of God in the places of our being where our truest desires and deepest longings stir. These discoveries are available to all of us as we become more *honest in naming what isn't working so that we can craft a way of life that is more congruent with our deepest desires…*[5]

As I read those words, a dream to live and lead from a life of greater health and wholeness was birthed in me. The desire to help other Christian leaders do the same started that day. This is something I've been pursuing and trying to live ever since. But first, I had to admit what I was currently experiencing in my own life and leadership wasn't working. Who I was becoming and what I was experiencing was incongruent with who I wanted to be, how I wanted to live, and what I wanted to accomplish. In short, my current state of life and leadership was unsustainable. There had to be better way.

So if you're willing to admit that what you're currently experiencing isn't working and isn't sustainable, and if you believe there's a healthier way to do life and leadership as a Christian leader, then *Staying Power:5 Core Ideas To Sustainability in Christian Leadership* is for you.

ACTION AND APPLICATION

Review the years of your leadership in Christian ministry. When were the good seasons? And why?

_____

_____

When were the difficult seasons? And why?

_____

_____

In what ways has your journey in Christian leadership affected your soul? _____

_____

What would you say is the current state of your soul?

_____

_____

RECOMMENDED RESOURCES:
- *Strengthening The Soul of Your Leadership* by Ruth Haley Barton
- *Leading on Empty* by Wayne Cordeiro
- *The Resilient Life* by Gordon Macdonald

CHAPTER TWO

LOOKING BELOW THE WATERLINE

What lies behind us and what lies before us are tiny matters compared to what lies within us.

Ralph Waldo Emerson

Michael Plant had already sailed solo around the world three times, so it was no special concern when he left New York Harbor on October 16th, 1992 and headed across the Atlantic for France. Once he arrived, his plan was to set sail again; this time as the only American competing against seventeen other sailors, in a non-stop, single-handed race around the world. Somewhere while crossing the Atlantic, something went wrong and America's most renowned solo sailor went missing. The Coast Guard launched one of the largest and longest rescue missions ever conducted in the North Atlantic. After a thirty day, 200,000 square mile air search, they suspended their efforts to find Michael Plant.

Four days later, an oil tanker spotted Plant's yacht, the *Coyote*, off the coast of France, capsized and drifting in eight foot seas. The yacht's mast, although plunging eighty-five feet into the cold water, was still rigged with her sails. The boat's carbon-fiber keel wasn't damaged, its twin rudders were operational and its hull was still intact. So what had happened to the *Coyote?* More importantly, what had happened to her captain?

After closer investigation, it was discovered that the 8,400 pound lead bulb that should have been attached to the bottom of the keel was missing. Without the weighted bulb stabilizing the keel, any considerable wind would capsize the yacht, making it a death trap to anyone on board.

How could this have happened? Conversations with Michael's family and friends offered a clue. What may have happened is that Michael was already behind schedule to get the new yacht sea worthy; somehow in the rush, the critical lead bulb may have been improperly installed. As a result, while America's most renowned and experienced solo sailor was crossing the Atlantic, a flaw just below the waterline was occurring, which eventually led to his death. Michael Plant, only days away from his 42nd birthday, was never found. [1]

Too often those of us in Christian leadership are similar to Michael Plant. We swiftly move through life unaware of what's happening just below the waterline, and although the outcome may not be as dramatic or as fatal, if left unattended, we too eventually pay the price.

EVALUATING WHAT WE'RE EVALUATING

It's unfortunate, but when we approach this discussion on the health and wholeness of a leader, and consider some keys to greater sustainability in ministry, we too often focus on areas above the waterline. We work on things more easily seen and more readily fixed; a new time management tool, better delegation techniques, improved communication, team building practices, and other efforts to strengthen our leadership and management skills. Many of these improvements are helpful, and no doubt needed. But, like taking an aspirin when an operation is needed, these modifications seldom go to the root issues, and as a result, they only provide partial, short-term solutions.

Unfortunately, one of the reasons we give more attention to issues above the waterline is because most of the accolades handed out in our profession are based on externals. We get applauded for what is seen. We get rewarded for what is measurable. Like Michael Plant, things that are unseen go unnoticed, and because they go unnoticed, they go unappreciated, and since they go unappreciated, they go unattended. As Jesus pointed out, why shine up the outside of the cup when the inside is left unkempt and unclean? (Matt. 23: 25- 26)

Through my own journey, I'm convinced that what's happening *in* us is the most important thing *about* us. The state of our soul – our inner world – is the incubator *for* and the indicator *of* our health as a spiritual leader. Yet, much of what's defined and celebrated as a *successful* Christian leader almost exclusively focuses on the external: the size of our congregation, the size of our building, the size of our budget. These metrics frequently determine where we are placed on the leadership ladder of success, which is unfortunate. My question is, what do any of these external metrics have to do with the state of our soul?

How many times have you – like me – been at a gathering with other Christian leaders when the conversation inevitably turns toward the inescapable question, "How big is your congregation?" Or a more subtle way to gain the same information, "So, hey man, uh like, how many people are on your staff?" The first thought that usually runs through my head isn't printable and the second more sanitized one is usually, "Hey dude, who cares and why does it even matter?!"

I've pastored both large and small congregations. I've led churches that were rapidly growing and others that were rapidly declining. Defining the health of a Christian leader by focusing on externals is like admiring a beautiful building from the outside, unaware that inside the walls are crumbling, and the basement is home to a deadly mold.

Despite the number of Christian leaders already piled up along the side of the road, it seems we still don't understand how important it is to cultivate a healthy inner life, or care for our own soul. Or maybe, it's that we honestly don't know how to do so?

One of the externals emphasized over the past few decades has been the topic of leadership. Numerous books on the subject have been written, and countless conferences have been attended. Areas like church growth, vision casting, strategic planning, the discipline of execution, the art of delegation, doing ministry in teams, effective communication, the use of the creative arts, and a host of other similar topics have been emphasized. Even as I sit in my office writing, I'm surrounded by many of my own books on the subject. A quick glance over my shoulder illustrates my point: *The 21 Irrefutable Laws of Leadership, Good to Great, Developing The Leader Within, The Leadership Engine, Courageous Leadership, Leadership That Works, The Power of Vision, Masterplanning, Twelve Keys to an Effective Church, Strategy For Leadership, Strength Finders, Leading Your Church to Growth, The Seven Laws of Christian Leadership, The Top Ten Mistakes Leaders Make,* and many other books on leadership line my shelves.

THE EXTERNAL TO INTERNAL RATIO

As Christian leaders, we have certainly benefited over the past few decades from training on leadership. There is no need to vilify one emphasis on leadership (external) to emphasis another (internal). Therefore I don't want to do that here. We need *skilled* leaders.

It's unfortunate, however, that during the same period of time in which the emphasis on leadership skills has surged (competence), the equal emphasis on the inner life of a leader (character) has seemingly waned. One Christian leader describes his experience with this external to internal ratio with these words, "For years I learned from leaders and consultants around the country *how* to lead a large, growing church. [Yet] None of the training I received concerned itself with *knowing myself*." [2]

A colleague and close friend recently related a story to me that further describes my point. My friend was asked to do a breakout session on the Health of a Christian Leader at a national leadership conference. The conference had over 6000 in attendance and offered hundreds of breakout sessions on every area of ministry within the church that you can think of. Only two breakout sessions were offered on the health of a Christian leader, and of the 6000 in attendance, only 17 attended my friend's session.

What's further revealing (and disturbing) is that while we've emphasized leadership skills, the reputation of Christian leaders hasn't increased, but actually decreased. According to some surveys, when compared to other vocations, our reputation is often placed somewhere near the bottom of the list – right next to used car salesmen, politicians, and lobbyists.

When my father began pastoring in 1963, it was an honorable profession. But today, when I'm introduced as a pastor, sometimes I cringe. It's a bit like politics; there are certain seasons when no one in their right mind wants to be associated with it. Not because Christian leadership isn't a high calling, but because it is! As Christian leaders we've done so many questionable and crazy things in our leadership and within the life of the church, that we've dishonored what God considers – and what others should consider – a very high and holy call.

The issue isn't that many of the books and seminars on leadership haven't emphasized the need for *character* in the life of a leader. But, too often, the *clarity* of what a healthy, spiritual leader really looks like or the *clear instruction* on exactly how to go about becoming one has had little emphasis. Like a dentist with rotting teeth, this neglect has been to our "profession's" own decline. If we are going to build a life of sustainability in Christian ministry, then one of the things we must do is take the time to go below the waterline of our lives and consider what's really happening in our inner world.

JESUS AND THE INNER LIFE

Jesus certainly understood the importance of below the waterline issues. Of course he didn't use that language, but on several occasions he did make the point that what's happening in a person's heart – what's happening in our inner world – is really the most important thing about us. Jesus knew that it's in our inner world where things germinate, and eventually surface. He helps us grasp this important truth by giving us some simple yet profound analogies. On one occasion he states, "A good tree will produce good fruit and a bad tree will produce bad fruit." He then continues by saying, "a good man will bring out good things stored up *in him* and a bad man will bring out the bad things stored up *in him* (Matthew 12:33-35).

In essence, Jesus is saying that it's impossible for a weeping willow to produce roses, or for the inner life of Adolph Hitler to produce the outer life of Mother Teresa. What's on the inside defines who we *really* are and determines who we will *eventually* become.

No one is exempt from this inner life to outer life reality – especially Christian leaders. In fact, we see Jesus challenging the religious leaders of his day to take a hard, honest look at below the waterline issues in their own lives. He confronts them with these rhetorical questions. Why would you clean the outside of the cup when the inside is filthy? Why would you put a fresh coat of paint on the outside of a tomb when a dead man is rotting on the inside? Since you are already bound up by religion, why would you go to such great lengths to bring others into the same bondage? If you can't find your own way, why lead others down the same blind path with you?

Jesus' words to the religious leaders of his day may seem harsh, but he knew the depth of their blindness and the strength of their denial. Therefore he realized that a two point sermon, with a poem and a few rosy words thrown in wouldn't do the job! A complete heart transplant was needed.

As Christian leaders, it's not a matter of *if* what's happening below the waterline will surface, it's only a question of *when*. Dallas Willard illustrates this inner life to outer life principle. He writes: "The 'sudden' failures that appear in the lives of some ministers...are never really sudden but are the surfacing of longstanding deficiencies in the 'hidden person of the heart' (I Peter 3:4)." [3] Another Christian leader says it this way; "Failing in the life of a leader is not a quick fall. Rather it's the consequence of a pattern of long concessions." [4] In essence, the same principle of sowing and reaping that applies to the agricultural world applies to our inner world. An oak tree doesn't surface in a day and a sinkhole doesn't develop overnight. Who you and I will be tomorrow, we are becoming that person today.

To those involved in Christian leadership, Jesus' teaching on this important inner life to outer life principle isn't new. In fact, most of us have quoted these same words, and taught the same principles that Jesus did. Unfortunately, many of the confessions of today's Christian leaders, and most of the statistics describing our current crisis suggest that we may be preaching these principles to others but not actually practicing them ourselves.

This may seem like a cruel indictment, but I honestly don't think that the gap between our external and internal lives is an intentional one. Most Christian leaders I know *want* to cultivate a healthy inner life, and they *want* to help those they serve do the same. If your journey is anything like mine, there are at least two challenges that work against living this kind of healthy inner life and leading others into it. These two challenges are a lack of training, and busyness.

A LACK OF TRAINING

My first challenge was a lack of training. Growing up in the church, it always bothered me when I was challenged to *do* something – be a better person, don't do that, do this, stop doing that, start doing this – without receiving clear and specific instructions on *how* to do it. It's like telling your teenage son to overhaul the engine of your car, when he's never even been taught how to change the oil. Being challenged to do something without being instructed on *how to do it* only causes frustration and discouragement. This often leads to passivity ("Why try?") or even worse, hypocrisy ("I'll just act like I know what I'm doing").

Although we've been trained in many aspects of our vocation, few of us have been trained in how to build a healthy inner life. Even though I grew up in church, graduated from a Christian seminary, and had been pastoring for over 20 years, I still lacked the clear and specific training I needed to care for my soul. I knew how to study the bible, how to prepare a sermon, how to chair a business meeting, how to perform marriages, how to conduct funerals, and the list goes on, but I'd never been taught how to tend to or how to cultivate my own inner world.

BUSYNESS

My second challenge was busyness. In 1978 Richard Foster in his book, *Celebration of Discipline* said "Superficiality is the curse of our age." Then in 1997 John Ortberg in his book *The Life You've Always Wanted* expanded on this idea with these words, "If *superficiality* is the curse of our age, then *hurry* pronounces the spell." [5] If this statement made by Richard Foster in 1978 and expanded on by John Ortberg in 1997 was true and relevant then, how much more true is it today?

We are moving at such high speeds, under such heavy loads, stimulated by stress and anesthetized by entertainment, that many of us don't have the foggiest idea what's happening in our inner world. It takes time and space to go below the waterline, to discover the *true* state of our soul, and make the needed adjustments. Yet, everything in our world runs fast and demands us to keep up. Tending to our inner life isn't a one minute management check-off item that can be done while hydroplaning through life with one hand on the open throttle and the other steering wildly. It's impossible to do significant inner life assessment with three phone calls on hold, our next appointment waiting outside the door, and ninety-seven emails that need a reply. It's difficult to go deep and fast at the same time. Therein lies our dilemma.

This doesn't mean that we are irresponsible or unproductive in our work. That isn't the issue. The question is, which side of the scale do we place the most weight? Inward or outward? Depth or speed? Authenticity or Activity? Public or Private?

Richard Foster further helps us with this inner to outer life equation. He writes,

Outwardly we are carrying on the task of our day: scrubbing floors, talking with clients, working at our computer. Yet underneath, deeper down, our life is hid with Christ in God. And it is here in *the innermost sanctuary of the soul* that the real, substantive work of spiritual formation goes on. How hard it is for us to value this *inward reality*, which remains out of sight to all but the most spiritually sensitive. The outward is clamoring and demanding. The inward is silent and never draws attention to itself. If we satisfy the outward we receive acclaim. If we satisfy the inward we receive nothing. Well, nothing outwardly – inwardly we experience a life of righteousness, peace and joy in the Holy Spirit. We must, however, remember that this is a 'double' motion. It isn't as if the outward is bad and the inward good. Oh, no! *It is that the inward is central and the outward flows out of the inward.* As we give attention to that which is central, the outward tasks of life become more like a reflex action to the prior initiation of the heart." [6]

Granted, we all have seasons of rapid pace with rewarding productivity. That's necessary and needed. External fruitfulness should be the natural result of inward faithfulness. That's a given. But the danger is in allowing the frenetic routine of our external activities to become the dominant rhythm of our life and leadership. If we allow this pattern to drive us for too long, our productivity may expand, but our soul will shrink.

Most Christian leaders I know aren't lazy or undisciplined. Just the opposite, they want to make a difference in people's lives. They want to respond to every need and call of service. Sometimes however, this desire to help everyone else ends up pulling us away from the very thing that's so essential – the awareness *of* and the attention *to* the shaping of our own inner world.

If Michael Plant had known what was happening just below the waterline, his tragedy could have been avoided. You and I have that opportunity. So let's take the time, dive a little deeper, and take a closer look.

ACTION AND APPLICATION

On a scale of 1 to 5 (1 High, 3 Average, 5 Low), how self-aware are you? Why or why not?

_____

_____

On a scale of 1 to 5, how healthy is your inner world? (1 High, 3 Average, 5 Low) Why or why not?

_____

_____

Which one these two is your greatest challenge to building a healthy inner life?

A Lack of Training   _____

Busyness   _____

What other challenge do you find in building a healthy inner life? Why?

_____

_____

RECOMMENDED RESOURCES:

- *Emotionally Healthy Spirituality* by Peter Scazzero
- *Strengthening the Soul of Your Leadership* by Ruth Haley Barton
- *Overcoming the Darker Side Of Leadership* by McIntosh and Rima

CHAPTER THREE

TRAVELERS BEWARE

Would you tell me, please, which way I ought to go from here?
ALICE IN WONDERLAND

Many years ago while visiting my in-laws in Canada, my wife and I made a spur of the moment decision to load our children on a greyhound bus and send them on a trip over the Canadian Rockies. Our kids hadn't been *that* unruly, we just wanted them to spend some time with their cousins who lived in the next province to the west. The following morning we took our daughter Nicole (14) and our son Britton (12) to the bus depot, bought them a one way ticket, and got them settled on the bus.

As the bus idled in the terminal waiting for other passengers to board, I remember pacing back and forth in front of the bus. I would stop, read the sign displaying its final destination, pace back and forth, stop and read the sign again – and like a beat cop repeat the pattern all over again. I still wasn't convinced of the bus's final destination, so I made my way up the first few steps, got the bus driver's attention and said, "Excuse me sir, uh, is this bus headed to British Columbia?" He assured me it was.

The problem wasn't that I couldn't read, nor was I being an overly protective, paranoid parent. I simply wanted to make sure that when this bus left the terminal in Calgary, Alberta, it would head west over the Canadian Rockies, and seven hours later arrive in Shuswap, British Columbia – the place of our desired destination. My fear was that I would get a phone call from my daughter later that night telling me through her tears, "Daddy we just got off the bus and we're not sure how it happened, but Daddy, we ended up in Las Vegas!"

The journey into our inner life can be, and for many has been, a perilous one. I'm very aware that, for many within the Christian community, any serious discussion on the subject makes us uneasy – and for good reason. Similar to my children's trip over the Rockies, knowing where we are headed *before* we start out is a wise thing to do. And it's especially true concerning our journey below the waterline of our lives.

So in this chapter I want to put you at ease by being clear on where we're not headed.

THE WORLD OF POP PSYCHOLOGY

First, we're not headed into the uncertain waters of pop psychology or down the path of the self-help movement. It's true, ideas like self-awareness and self-discovery are more associated with secular psychology than Christian theology. And it's true, historically these topics have been more associated with names like Carl Rogers, Sigmund Freud, and Abraham Maslow than names like John Owens, John Calvin, or Jesus Christ. Therefore, for those of us who embrace an orthodox Christian theology, heading down this journey of self-discovery or self-awareness gives us legitimate caution and concern.

As Christians, it is our conviction that much of the secular, self-help, pop psychology, presents the belief that the potential for change and the power for man's greatness lies *solely* within our own mastering. Admittedly, this is a belief system that is fundamentally different from our own.

Christian theologian John Stott, warns us of the erroneous belief of the self-help movement with these words, "The New Age Movement (and the Human Potential Movement) calls us to look inside ourselves, to explore ourselves, for the solution to our problems is within. [This movement suggests] We do not need a savior to come to us from somewhere else; *we can be our own savior.*" [1]

Ideas like self-awareness and self-discovery, haven't only been used as a means to pursue man's greatest potential, they've also been a means to defend some of man's greatest depravities. Labels like self-discovery and self-realization have been used, and are still being used, to justify some of man's most extreme acts of selfish hedonism and unbridled narcissism. In some cases, these same labels are used to explain and excuse people's acts of deviant behavior.

For example, pedophiles are trying to legitimize having sex with children on the basis that their sexual desire for children is "just who they are," and "how they are made." And some psychiatrists are joining their fight. [2]

This is an extreme example, but it proves my point. Many appalling acts have been, and are being, committed under the guise, "I've just got to be me," or with the flippant justification, "that's just who I am!"

This misguided idea of self-discovery reminds me of a Christian book published a number of years ago titled, *I Gotta Be Me*. Although there is some truth to the book's title, it's important to determine what "me" I've got to be! A "me" designed by obsessive and egotistical desires, or a "me" defined by a narcissistic and neurotic culture, probably isn't the person I want to discover or the person I need to be.

As one Christian professor of psychology writes,

> It is a profound irony to write a book promoting self-discovery to people who are seeking to follow a self-sacrificing Christ. It might make you fear that I have forgotten – or worse, failed to take seriously – Jesus' paradoxical teaching that it is in *losing* our self that we truly *find* it (Matthew 10:39). ... While concepts such as self-discovery, identity and authenticity are easily dismissed as mere psychobabble, each has an important role to play in the transformational journey of Christian spirituality. Even in the Matthew passage just referenced, Jesus talks as much about self-discovery as self-sacrifice! But there is no question that the journey of finding our truly authentic self *in Christ* and rooting our identity *in this reality* is dramatically different from the agenda of self-fulfillment promoted by pop psychology. [3]

From a Christian perspective, we *do* acknowledge that *some* insights from psychology, and some of the other social sciences, are certainly helpful. Yet, we also maintain that any help left *only* to self-help is, in the end, incomplete. In some cases, it's little to no help at all. As Christians, we believe remedies for health and wholeness are found both within us *and* from a "source" beyond us.

THE CHURCH WORLD

If the first reason for caution and concern comes from the world of pop psychology, then the second reason comes from the church world. Let me explain.

When I write about embarking on an authentic journey into our inner world, I'm not suggesting we sit in a circle holding hands, singing Kumbaya and pointing out each other's weaknesses. Nor am I suggesting a navel-gazing, self-groveling religious exercise that leads to condemnation. Promoting hyper sensitivity to the slightest hint of our every possible sin, or preaching an obsessive introspection toward our every questionable motive isn't the life of freedom that Jesus came to give. Yet sadly, some segments of the Church have used this idea of evaluating the state of our soul as a way to preach perpetual guilt and keep their constituents captive to their own religious systems of control and bondage.

This overemphasis on introspection leading to perpetual guilt isn't limited to the Catholic arm of the Church. It's also a ploy applied in some expressions of the Evangelical church. By overemphasizing sin, certain segments have implemented the same systems of bondage, just in different forms. Some, using the doctrine of depravity and what has historically been known as the doctrine of indwelling sin, have created their own religious systems of guilt and shame as a way to keep their constituents captive to their own forms of pious bondage.

I know of a church planting movement who many years ago started exerting a heavy handed top-down authority, which eventually ended up as spiritual abuse. One of the ways they did this was by using an overemphasis on the doctrine of indwelling sin to shame anyone who disagreed with them. In reality, this was just a way to coerce and keep many of their congregants in check. I'm not sure it was their intent, but nonetheless, many people were damaged in its wake.

Neither of these extremes represent the life of forgiveness or the gospel of grace that Jesus came to give. In reality, this is just another form of slavery with a religious bow tied around it. Therefore, for many of us who've grown up in the church, when we start talking about evaluating our inner life, it brings up a legitimate caution and a valid concern. If you've already been down a shame-based and guilt-ridden religious road, then, like me, you have no interest in heading down it again.

A BALANCED AND BIBLICAL APPROACH

It's important, however, that we don't overreact to these past or present examples of misuse or abuse, but instead, introduce and practice the proper use. There are certainly numerous places throughout the Bible that instruct us to be aware of the inner workings of our heart and to know the true state of our soul.

• "Search me, O God, and *know my heart*; test me

and know my anxious thoughts. See if there is any offensive way *in me*, and lead me in the way ever-lasting." Psalms 139: 23 and 24

- "Surely you desire truth *in the inner parts...*" Psalms 51: 6
- "His speech is smooth as butter yet war is *in his heart.*" Psalms 55:21
- "Test me, O Lord, and try me, *examine my heart and my mind;*" Psalms 26:2

Scriptures that encourage us to be aware of what's happening in our inner world aren't limited to a few, random passages found in the Old Covenant. The same encouragement for inner assessment is found throughout the pages of the New Covenant.

- "Put to death impurity, lust, evil desires, greed, anger, rage, malice..." Colossians 3: 5-8
- "Get rid of all bitterness, rage and anger, brawling and slander, along with every form of malice..." Ephesians 4:31-5:7
- "... put off pride and put on humility." I Peter 5:5 and 6
- "My conscience is clear, but that does not make me innocent. It is the Lord who judges me. ...He will bring to light what is hidden in darkness and will expose the motives of men's hearts." I Corinthians 4: 4-5

Again, there is a balance here. It's important we don't

become so introspective that we negate the very heart of the gospel. By grace we are forgiven. By the work of the cross we are a new creation. We have a new nature and a new life of freedom. It's just as important that we don't move to the other extreme, where under the guise of grace or the safety of eternal security, we're oblivious to the destructive seeds germinating in our heart, or blind to the fatal flaws functioning just below the waterline of our lives.

It's my observation that in most segments of the Church we are fairly clear on the doctrine of grace (there are some exceptions). Unfortunately, we don't seem to be as comfortable with the penetrating work of God's Word, which empowered by the Holy Spirit, works its way, into the dark and deceptive places of our heart, and like a miner's lamp, brings to light what's really there.

Instead, we primarily focus on the more obvious and overt acts of sin, while the more subtle, yet just as dangerous and damaging impulses of our heart, we naively and conveniently avoid. Admittedly, external acts like sexual immorality, drunkenness, and murder are much easier to spot than internal ones like envy, ambition, and idolatry. Yet, the Bible considers the latter group as damaging and deadly as the former. I don't know how many times I've seen people shamed and shunned for committing adultery, while those who do the shaming are themselves gluttons who, like garlic, reek of pride, anger and envy. Aren't both guilty?

Similar to groping around in a dimly lit cave, our inner world can be a shadowy place to explore. Once we enter, like Alice in Wonderland, we may be afraid of what we'll find, or be concerned we may never find our way out again. However, if we are ever going to be healthy and whole and build a life of staying power in Christian ministry – enter in we must!

A BIBLICAL AND HISTORICAL PRECEDENT

Both Jesus and the Apostle Paul encouraged us to enter into our inner world. Although they didn't use that language, they did emphasize the importance of knowing the condition of our heart.

Jesus repeatedly challenged his disciples, as well as his distractors, to take an honest look *on the inside* and discover who they really were (Matt. 12:33-35; Matt. 23:1-32). In fact, much of what Jesus taught in the Sermon on the Mount had to do with going beyond external acts and evaluating what's happening in our inner world (Matthew 5: 21- 30). According to Jesus, it's easy to identify the act of murder but much more difficult to discern the anger idling in our own heart. Or as he pointed out, it's easy to point the finger at someone else's act of adultery but it's much more difficult to admit our own impure urges. With these two examples, Jesus is making it quite clear that, without an awareness of what's transpiring in our heart, no real repentance *can* occur. And without real repentance, no authentic transformation *will* occur.

The apostle Paul understood this same principle. Paul knew who he *once* was, and because of the transforming power of the gospel, who he *now* was (I Timothy 1:15; Ephesians 3:8; I Corinthians 15: 9 – 10). Paul understood that because of the work of the cross and the work of grace, he was a new creation. But he was also aware of his *ongoing inner struggle*

(Romans 7:7-25; II Corinthians 4:7-12; II Corinthians 7:5 – 13; I Timothy 1: 19 – 20). In addition, Paul, in his writings, warns his readers about the deceptive and destructive ways of inner motives (sin) like anger, envy, malice, jealousy, greed, and pride. Just as Paul encouraged the early church to be aware of and deal with these inner issues of the heart, he calls us in the Church to do the same today (Ephesians 4:17 – 5:7; Colossians 3:5-10; I Corinthians 6: 9 – 10; Galatians 5: 16 – 26; Romans 6: 1 – 19 and many others).

This encouragement to consider what's happening below the waterline of our life wasn't only taught by Jesus and the Apostle Paul (although that should be sufficient). Throughout the history of the church, many other leading voices have reinforced this idea.

- Augustine, one of the most influential figures in church history, prayed this prayer, "Grant Lord, that I may *know myself* that I may know thee." [4]
- Thomas á Kempis, in his fifteenth century work *The Imitation of Christ* made this assertion, "a humble *self-knowledge* is a surer way to God than a search after deeper learning. [5]
- John Calvin, one of the greatest thinkers in the history of the church opens his remarkable work, *The Institutes of the Christian Religion* with these words, "There is no deep knowing of God without a deep *knowing of self* and no deep knowing of self without a deep knowing of God." [6]
- And the great Puritan writer, John Owen, in

his classic work *Sin and Temptation*, writes these profound words on our need for greater self-knowledge and self-awareness.

> Many men live in the dark to themselves all their days. Whatever else they know, *they know not themselves*. Indeed few labor to grow wise in this matter. Few study themselves as they ought, (or) are acquainted with the evils of their own hearts as they ought. This then is our wisdom, to repair these omissions and to get to *know ourselves* and to know in particular what damage sin is seeking to do in our spiritual and moral system. [7]

Indeed, from both pop psychology and the history of the church, the journey into the inner life has been littered with many land mines. Certainly, some who've started out on this journey have arrived at undesired destinations. Therefore, it is with some legitimate caution and concern that we begin this journey. However, one thing is sure – despite the danger or discomfort; if we are going to live a life of greater health and wholeness, and build a life of sustainability in Christian ministry, then, enter in we must!

ACTION AND APPLICATION

Does this topic of "the inner life" or self-discovery give you caution and concern? If so, why or why not?

_____

_____

Have you ever had a bad experience with the world of pop psychology or the self-help movement? If so, when and why?

_____

_____

Have you ever had a bad experience in the Church world with shame based guilt or forms of spiritual abuse? When and how?

_____

_____

Do you believe, as I've proposed in this chapter, that what's happening in us may be the most important thing about us?

_____

_____

RECOMMENDED RESOURCES:

- *The Biblical View of Self-Esteem, Self-Love, Self-Image* by Jay E. Adams
- *The Gift of Being Yourself* by David G. Benner

CHAPTER FOUR

PRETENDING AS A PROFESSION

Performance is where we try to make an impression
rather than just be what we are.

DALLAS WILLARD

John is desperate for work so he goes to a zoo where he's heard of some job openings. He strolls past the monkey house, stops and looks at the lions, and proceeds past the polar bears. Tucked away behind the maintenance building, he finds the employment office. Jim, the zoo keeper, personnel director *and* owner, greets him at the door. John extends his hand and says, "Hello, I'm John and I'm interested in a job here at the zoo." Jim clears his throat, shakes John's hand and says, "Good to meet you, but uh, unfortunately the only job still available is for someone who's willing to dress up in a gorilla suit and act like a gorilla." (OK, so the story's not true, but stay with me. It has a good punch line and it makes an important point.) John says, "What? Can you repeat that?" Jim says, "Sure. Uh, sorry, but the only job still available is for someone who's willing to dress up in a gorilla suit, crawl into the gorilla cage and act like a gorilla."

Since John really needs a job (and has been known to have long lapses in sound judgment) he says, "OK, I'll do it." Enthusiastically, Jim shakes John's hand hands him a liability waiver and says "Fill this out, leave it on my desk and you can start first thing in the morning." The next day John shows up bright and early, suits up, crawls into the gorilla cage, and to the delight of the crowd – starts acting like a gorilla.

He loves his new job. Within weeks, he's really got the hang of this gorilla gig. Then, one day while swinging on a rope and getting a bit *too* much into pretending, John swings right over the top of his cage and lands in the adjacent one. As soon as his feet hit the ground, he feels the hot breath of some beast breathing down his neck. He wheels. A ferocious lion is staring him in the face. John panics. He starts running in circles, screaming "Help! Help! Let me out of here! I'm not a gorilla. I'm a human and my name is John. Oh, please, please, somebody, get me out of here!" The lion pounces, pushing him to the ground, and just when John thinks he's about to be devoured, the lion whispers, "Oh, shut up you fool or we'll both be without a job!"

This story, although obviously fictional, still makes the factual point: *trying to be someone we are not can be dangerous.*

OUR PROPENSITY TO PRETEND

Once we start out on this journey and decide to take a look below the waterline of our lives, what exactly is it we're looking for? Of course we're looking for the obvious: hidden sin, patterns of compromise, places in our soul where slow and subtle erosion is already at work. We're also searching for something more. We're looking for areas where we're pretending to be someone we're not. Some call this "posing." Others call it play acting. Some call it living from a false self. Jesus called it what it is; hypocrisy.

Let's be honest, all of us pretend. We are insecure, but act confident. We are proud, but feign humility. We are fearful, but fake courage. A colleague once described to me a person he was counseling as someone who on the outside presented herself like a swan; very calm and composed, gliding smoothly over the water. But, he said, in reality, on the inside she was really more like a duck, who just below the waterline was frantically paddling in every direction.

John Eldredge, in his breakthrough book, *Wild At Heart*, unveils the reality of how men and women *both* hide and pretend. He writes,

> Adam knows now that he has blown it, that something has gone wrong within him, that he is no longer what he was meant to be. Adam doesn't just make a bad decision; he gives away something essential to his nature. He is marred now, his strength is fallen, and he knows it. Then what happens? *Adam hides*: 'I was afraid because I was naked; so I hid' (Gen. 3:10). You don't need a course in psychology to understand men [or women].
>
> …We are all hiding, every last one of us. Well aware that we, too, are not what we were meant to be, desperately afraid of exposure, terrified of being seen

for what we are and *are not*, we have run off into the bushes. We hide in our office, at the gym, behind the newspaper and mostly behind our personality. Most of what you encounter when you meet a man is a façade, an elaborate fig leaf, a brilliant disguise. [1]

It's true. In one way or another – whether male or female and with whatever fig leaf we choose to do so – we all hide. Therefore any authentic journey toward greater health and wholeness will inevitably uncover areas where we're hiding; ways we're pretending to be someone we're not.

The Christian psychologist, David Benner, in his excellent book *The Gift Of Being Yourself*, gives us great insight into how all of us hide and pretend. He writes:

Generally transformational knowing of self always involves encountering and embracing previously un-welcomed parts of self. While we tend to think of ourselves as a single, unified self, what we call "I" is really a family of many part-selves. That in itself is not a particular problem. The problem lies in the fact that many of these part-selves are unknown to us. Even though they are usually known to others, we remain blissfully oblivious of their existence.

To say that we are a family of many part-selves is not the same as saying that we play different roles. Most of us know what it is to be a friend, employee, church member, and possibly a parent or a spouse. Each of these roles is different, and most of us can move between them effortlessly. This is not the problem.

The problem is that there are important aspects of our experience we ignore. They make us feel too vulnerable. *So we pretend* they do not exist and hope they will go away. Or it may be our broken and wounded self that we try to deny. When we do so, however, these unwanted parts of self do not go away. *They simply go hiding.* [2]

As Christian leaders, pretending to be someone we're not is pretty standard practice. Whether we hide behind a suit, a robe, a pulpit, a title, a corner office, or God – we all have our fig leaves. It's unfortunate, but in our need for approval and our search for significance many of us play so many parts behind so many painted masks that sometimes we honestly may not know who we really are.

I recently heard one of my colleagues sarcastically confess, "I've become so good at my own 'impression management' that I've actually impressed myself." (I think that's called self-deception!) Admittedly, some of us have more self-delusion than others, but, like bad breath, we all have it to some degree. Our pretending can become so permanent that it's difficult to distinguish the "performer" from the person. Is it Superman or Clark Kent? Is it Batman or Bruce Wayne? Is it *The Reverend* Kenneth L. Roberts or is it Ken Roberts?

In my thirty plus years of pastoring, I've been in far too many gatherings with other Christian leaders where the political posturing and professional pretending has been as obvious – and overwhelming – as the smell of cheap cologne at a high school prom. If we ever got past all the professional preliminaries, and finally got around to talking about our personal lives and how we're *really* doing, I either got a blank stare or the ongoing standard perfunctory, professional pastors' speak; which usually goes something like,

"I pastor such-and-such-church and my life consists of prayer, bible study, and leading religious meetings. Overall I'm doing well, my church is doing great, and God has certainly been faithful" (at least that last phrase is true!).

You know what's really rumbling about in their head (because it's rumbling around in mine), and what they really want to say is something like,

"My church is struggling and I'm really concerned about my spouse's emotional health. I'm also worried about some bad decisions and questionable company my teenage son is keeping. Just last night I lay awake thinking about how to pay my bills and wondering if I could ever get hired at another church. In all honesty, I'm not sure I can keep doing what I'm doing but I'm not sure what else to do."

Of course we seldom confess such things but instead pretend we have it all together and "Praise God! Everything is just fine!" Many times I've walked away from these gatherings wondering if a *real* person was even present.

AN ESSENTIAL FIRST STEP

I'm not trying to be harsh or arrogant, but as a fellow traveler, I'm convinced that until we're willing to embrace the reality that all of us are prone to pretend, we won't take this first crucial step toward honest self-awareness. Without this first step, it's impossible to build a healthy inner life, which is essential for a life of sustainability in Christian ministry.

Our ongoing denial that an imposter may make up part of our leadership persona only perpetuates our pretending and keeps the gorilla suit snug and secure. And I must candidly confess that, over my many years in ministry, I've seen a lot of grown men and women walking around the church in gorilla suits.

Are we willing to take this first step and acknowledge we're pretending? Are we willing to embrace humility and come out of hiding? That's the question.

Ruth Haley Barton, one of the current voices encouraging Christian leaders toward greater health and wholeness, writes of this essential first-step. "We long for more in our spiritual lives, that's for sure, but I'm not sure we're ready for the harrowing journey of death to the false self that any true spiritual journey entails." [3] Brennan Manning, in his book, *The Ragamuffin Gospel,* says it this way, "In order to free the captive, one must first name the captivity." [4] Jesus summed it up when he said, "You shall know the truth {even about yourself} and the truth shall set you free." [5] I think Harriet Tubman, the African American abolitionist, may have said it best: "I led a thousand slaves to freedom. I could have led a thousand more – if only they would have known they weren't free." [6] Wow!

Sheila Walsh, at the time a well-known Christian singer, writer, and cohost of the popular Christian T.V. show, *The 700 Club*, tells how she came face-to-face with her pretending. She writes:

> "One morning I was sitting on national television with my nice suit and inflatable hairdo and that night I was in the locked ward of a psychiatric hospital. It was the kindest thing God could have done to me."
>
> The very first day in the hospital, the psychiatrist asked me, "Who are you?"
>
> "I'm the co-host of *The 700 Club*."
>
> "That's not what I meant," he said.
>
> "Well, I'm a writer. I'm a singer."
>
> "That's not what I meant. Who are you?"
>
> "I don't have a clue," I said.
>
> And he replied, "Now that's right and that's why you're here." [7]

MY GORILLA SUIT

I remember the day one of my own imposters was uncovered. I was attending a men's conference at our church with a few hundred other men and had just heard a teaching about "posing" – pretending to be someone we're not. After the speaker finished his talk, he asked us to consider any areas where we might be posing, and if we found any, to go deeper and try to identify the reason(s) for our pretending.

The exercise was difficult for me. It wasn't that like everyone else, I didn't at times pretend to be someone I wasn't. But, because I had grown up in a fairly healthy, functional family, I couldn't pinpoint any particular events that had traumatized me and turned me into a pretender.

I hadn't experienced any abuse growing up (well, a good whooping now and again, but that didn't seem to damage me too much?). I wasn't aware of any dark, family secrets (if there are, they're still in the closet?). All of my six siblings turned out *fairly* normal (of course with a few of them, only time will tell?).

So as I sat rummaging through my memories and reflecting over my rather idyllic *Leave It To Beaver* life, I couldn't trace any trauma that might be the cause of my pretending. Then, like a curtain slowly opening across a stage, the Holy Spirit began to graciously unveil a major play actor in my life – one that had walked on stage at a very early age.

As a child, I made my bed, took out the trash, helped in the garden, mowed the yard, and finished the many chores my dad seemed to find for me. I seldom got in trouble (I left that to my younger brother Carl). I was generally a kind and respectful kid, and I dutifully addressed the adults in my life with "yes sir" and "no sir," "yes mam" and "no mam."

As a student, I paid attention in class, did my homework and went beyond what was required of me. I made the honor roll and graduated in the top of my class.

As an athlete, I was diligent and disciplined. From my pee-wee sports teams all the way through my college years, I was selected a team captain. In college I played point guard on the basketball team, in which my main responsibility was to get the ball down the court, read the opposing team's defense, and call the right offensive plays.

But what I didn't realize during those developmental stages of my childhood and early adolescence, was that much of my identity was being secured *from* and being shaped *by* my reputation of *being responsible*. In many ways, I was already putting on a gorilla suit and didn't even know it.

Getting involved in pastoral ministry only reinforced the power of this imposter. In fact, in the city where I pastored for over twenty-five-years, I became known by many of my colleagues as a leader who could "handle a lot of responsibility." Many of my parishioners have said to me over and over again, "Pastor, how do you do it? You certainly carry a lot of responsibility." One of my closest colleagues once described himself as someone who wakes up every morning thinking "What do I *get* to do today?" He then described me as someone who wakes up every morning thinking "What do I *have* to do today?" He said he was a "get to guy" and I was an "ought to guy." Sadly, his description of me was true.

Over the years, being *the responsible* Christian leader became my calling card. Although I didn't realize it at the time, it was through this reputation that I gained many positions of influence, secured most of my significance, and acquired much of my approval. Of course, once my reputation as "a responsible Christian leader" had been built, I had to keep the image going. If I didn't, I might be accused of being irresponsible. I certainly couldn't live with that. So I worked harder, kept all the plates spinning, and continued holding up the world with one hand as I polished my Atlas image with the other.

But the world was getting real heavy.

I remember coming home from the office one day feeling

overwhelmed by the responsibilities of leading a large and growing congregation. There were so many things to do. Programs to plan. Problems to solve. People to please. As I stood in the living room gazing out our bay window, I watched my four year old son playing in the driveway. It had just rained and like most little boys his age, he quickly found his way to the puddles collected on the driveway. He jumped in; the water splashed up his legs. He jumped out; looked around to see if anyone was watching. He jumped in and jumped out; looked around. He jumped in and jumped out – the entire time grinning (and I'm sure with a deep giggle gurgling from his gut). As I watched I distinctly remember contrasting his joy of life with mine. Regrettably, the difference was achingly evident. As C.S. Lewis once wrote, "God wants a child's heart but a grown up head." [8] During that season of my life, it seemed I had lost both.

Granted, in most cases *being responsible* is a commendable trait. Therefore to some, defining it as an imposter may seem overstated. But, what I hadn't realized, until that moment of illumination at our men's retreat, was that this character trait, although laudable, had become my *primary identity*.

As I sat on the floor, surrounded by other men who were also thinking about where they might be pretending, I wrote these words:

> I'm turning fifty in a few weeks, and with it being almost three years since my late wife's passing, plus with all the conflict our church and pastoral team is going through, I'm being forced to consider areas where I've been posing. With the fundamental shift

I'm experiencing about living from the inside out, it seems that my responsibilities as a pastor is incongruent with the kind of authentic inner life that I want.

These two elements – my inner life and the responsibilities of my outer life – are warring against each other. Pastoring is doing damage to my heart – obligations, expectations, responsibilities, performances, conflict, tension, failure, wounds – all of these things are pushing against the deeper and more authentic part of me that's struggling to surface. The person I want to be is shouting to emerge.

I must make some changes so that my external life can match up with what's taking shape in my inner life. As a senior pastor, can the real me surface and survive? This question scares me. But it's a question I must ask and honestly answer. I either have to change the way I'm pastoring or no longer pastor. The health of my soul depends upon it.

I knew the change wouldn't be immediate, or come about by making a few easy, external modifications. Authentic change isn't like adjusting the side mirrors on your car. It doesn't work that way. It takes time. Authentic change has to work its way from the inside out.

It took intentional and intense effort, but eventually I stopped feeling responsible to have all the right answers for all the right people. How did I do that? I learned to more frequently and freely say "NO." I started taking my day off more regularly and I even began taking extended times away from my ministry responsibilities. But probably my biggest internal change was when I stopped playing Atlas and started trusting God to run the universe. Gradually, my approach to life and leadership changed. Eventually, I peeled away my gorilla suit – and oh what freedom I found!

LEADING OURSELVES BEFORE LEADING OTHERS

In reality, the journey of greater self-awareness is crucial for everyone. But, in many ways, it's even more crucial for Christian leaders. How can we lead others with clarity and courage unless we first know who we are? Isn't it impossible to lead others into health and wholeness unless, to some significant degree, we have come into this same place ourselves?

Once again the insight of Christian psychologist David Benner is helpful here. He writes, "We have focused on knowing God and tended to ignore knowing ourselves. The consequences have often been grievous – marriages betrayed, families destroyed, ministries shipwrecked and endless numbers of people damaged. ... Focusing on God while failing to know ourselves deeply may produce an external form of piety, but it will always leave a gap between appearance and reality. This is dangerous to the soul of anyone – and in spiritual leaders it can also be disastrous for those they lead." [9]

I agree with Dr. Benner. If you look close enough at some leaders whose lives have been shipwrecked, you'll usually find that these failures are often, but not always, the result of this one central issue: we do not know who we really are! Certainly, our sin nature and the many temptations that accompany sin play a role. And, certainly we have an enemy who plots his own schemes against us. *But, if you dig deep enough, you'll find that the root issue* (which provides the hook for temptation and the door for our enemy's entrance) *is often the uncertainty of our identity.* We are confused about *who* we are and *whose* we are. As a result, we build our lives and leadership on false identities. When the inevitable pressures from life and leading come, our false images fracture, and like a high-rise in the center of the city, if we do fall, we not only hurt ourselves, but also those we love and those we lead.

The reasons I pretend may not be the same reasons you pretend. The areas of my inner world that need to be reshaped may be different from your own. Whatever the areas, and for whatever the reasons, we must shed our gorilla suits and take the necessary steps to move into a life of greater health and wholeness. Our health, the health of our families, and the health of those we serve depend upon it.

ACTION AND APPLICATION

Have you experienced any major tragedy or trauma in your life that could be the cause for pretending?

_____

_____

Are there certain situations in your life or leadership that cause you to put on a gorilla suit?

_____

_____

Have you ever discovered areas where you were pretending? If so, how were you pretending and why were you pretending? And how did you come into a place of greater health and wholeness?

_____

_____

_____

_____

RECOMMENDED RESOURCES:
• _Emotionally Healthy Spirituality_ by Peter Scazzero
• _The Gift Of Being Yourself_ by David G. Benner

CHAPTER FIVE

WHY ARE WE SO SICK?

*The deepest form of despair
is to choose to be another than oneself.*

Søren Kierkegaard

On an overcast morning, in the early 1800's, Dr. William Morton began what would become a historic operation. He located the damaged organ, made the necessary cuts, and removed the appendix. The patient experienced some discomfort, but the pain quickly passed. The incision was sutured, the patient was checked, and the operation was considered a success.

Dr. Morton wasn't new to surgery, but this one was different – so different that it's recorded in medical history.

Dr. Morton was first trained in dentistry, and later trained as a doctor, but he was best known as a pioneer in anesthesiology.

As a dentist, his first notable procedure was using ether as an anesthetic. As history records it, when Dr. Morton finished pulling the patient's tooth using only ether as an anesthetic, he had his patient sign an affidavit stating "the tooth was pulled painlessly." The following day, the account of the "painless tooth extraction" appeared in the Boston Daily Journal. As you might expect, a hoard of people hurried to Dr. Morton's dental office.

Dr. Morton wasn't satisfied with using ether only in the dental chair, so sixteen days later in a medical procedure he tried his magic again. As colleagues, surgeons, and medical students looked on, Dr. Morton, again using ether as his only means of anesthetic, painlessly removed a tumor from the neck of a patient. [1]

Since he had performed many surgeries, both as dentist and doctor, then why was the appendectomy performed on that overcast morning considered so noteworthy? There were two reasons. First, it was the first time ether had been used as an anesthetic and the patient had successfully recovered; therefore, the operation was considered a major breakthrough in the field of anesthesiology. Second, Dr. Morton had tried, but couldn't convince anyone to let him operate on them using ether as the only form of anesthetic; so he took a more desperate route – he operated on himself.

If, as Christian leaders, we are ever going to cure ourselves of false images and build a greater foundation for sustainability in ministry, then like Dr. Morton, we too must be willing to operate on ourselves. Like any good doctor, before we begin wielding a sharp scalpel or dolling out medication, we should at least have some idea about the source of our sickness. And it's to that topic that we turn in this chapter.

SOME SOURCES TO OUR SOUL'S SICKNESS

Why is it that so many of our stories, and most of the statistics show that the longer we are involved in ministry, the greater tendency it is for our soul to be sick? Or, a more pointed way to ask the same question, why does Christian ministry seem to make so many of us so sick?

I've pondered this question for several years. I've examined my own leadership journey for some of the sources of my soul's sickness, and surveyed several of my colleagues about some of their own. My search has led me to four common sources in Christian ministry that often do damage to our soul: expectations, criticism, disappointment in dealing with people, and disappointment with God.

EXPECTATIONS

The amount of expectations that people put on Christian leaders, no matter how dedicated or skilled a leader may be, are beyond anyone's ability to fully perform. A basic list of these expectations usually includes, but is not limited to: a visionary and strategic leader, an engaging and entertaining communicator, a skilled and effective CEO, a kind and capable manager, an intelligent and in-depth scholar, a wise and compassionate counselor, a motivating and masterful team leader, a fundraiser and financial manager, a peacemaker, and a person of prayer. Oh, and on top of all of that, we're expected to be an exemplary spouse, a model parent, *and* a humble-servant-leader with impeccable Christian character. Who could ever fulfill that list of expectations? And who would even want to try? Just reading the list makes me twitch.

Every Christian leader knows the voice of these endless expectations. "Do this." "Don't do that." "Fix this." "Leave that alone." "We need this." "No, we don't need that." "We like this." "No, we don't like that." Sometimes responding to these expectations can make us feel more like a teenager on roller skates working at a car hop than a shepherd who's trying to shape the eternal souls of those we serve. I know of one pastoral team that sarcastically described the continual and unrealistic demands placed on them from the congregation in which they served as "being should-ed on."

In all honesty, it's not only the expectations others place on us that can do damage to our soul, but it's the expectations we place on ourselves. I know several Christian leaders who chronically deal with various strains of competitive compulsions, perfection disorders, and approval addictions. I know others who routinely deal with the ever present performance disease. I'm being a little facetious here (kind of), and for the sake of humor, using some hyperbole, but you get the point.

In addition to these occupational illnesses, many of us suffer from our own "internal demons of driveness." Sometimes we are driven by the whip of legalism, and at other times our own ambition. Sometimes we are driven by our need for approval, and at other times by our need for success. I find it ironic that, as Christian leaders, we religiously defend the doctrine of grace, while much of the time we faithfully function from the demands of the law.

We preach freedom but live out of duty.

Many of us live and lead as if a heavenly task master is looking over our shoulder (sometimes it's called a church board), meticulously keeping score of everything we do, or don't do. We feel that *enough* never is, and if we don't keep peddling really fast someone is going to pull the cord on the curtain we're hiding behind, and discover that the little man (or woman) sitting there isn't the person they're pretending to be. I know this scenario is true among many Christian leaders, because at one time or another I've been plagued by most of these occupational illnesses. And more than once, I've been the person cowering behind the curtain.

Over time, the expectations from others, as well as our own, can throw us into confusion concerning who we really are. A friend that I've known since we were roommates in Bible College (over forty years ago), recently confessed to me, "I had been pastoring for over twenty years and was in my mid-forties before I finally became comfortable with who I am and who I'm not. Up to that point in my life, I silently compared myself to many of my fellow pastors and covertly competed with most of them. I would beat myself up for not having the same level of giftedness, or the same level of fruitfulness, or the same level of recognition, or the same level of something… that many of my colleagues had. It wasn't until I accepted who God had made *me* to be, and embraced the level of gifting God had given *me*, that I finally came to a place of peace in my own soul and to a point of contentment in the place where I currently serve." Undoubtedly, many of us could make the same confession.

CRITICISM

Sadly, many of the expectations we experience are also accompanied by constant criticism. As one Christian leader noted, "As a leader of a Christian organization, I feel the brunt of just this kind of meanness within the Christian community, a mean-spirited suspicion and judgment that mirrors the broader culture. Every Christian leader I know feels it....It is difficult to be Christian in a secular world....But, you know, it is sometimes *more difficult* to be a leader in Christian circles. There too you can be vilified for just the slightest move that is displeasing to someone." [2]

As leaders, most of us would agree that some of the criticisms we've received are justly deserved. Many times, though, criticism can be hurled at us for the slightest and silliest of reasons. I know a pastor who recently got criticized for changing the kind of bread his congregation was using for communion. (Now think about the irony of that. While participating in the greatest sacrifice ever made on our behalf, we are complaining about something as insignificant as the type of wafer used for communion. There's something terribly wrong with that picture.) No matter how mature or dedicated a leader may be, if these endless expectations and cruel criticisms are left unchecked and unchallenged, they will, like plaque built-up in our arteries, do damage to our soul.

In fact, studies show that many Christian leaders – due to the endless expectations and constant criticism they've carried, and the damage it's done to their soul – have had to get out of ministry just to save their soul. And there are more lining up every day to do the same. Many leaders have found that their identities have become so confused, and their sense of self-worth so damaged, that in an attempt to rediscover who they really are, and return to some semblance of sanity, they have to leave the ministry, and go sell used cars or life insurance. No offense to car salesmen or insurance agents, but that's just sad.

One survey reported that 70% of pastors admit they have a lower self-image *after* serving for only a short time in ministry than before they started out.[3] And, according to an article in the New York Times, many clergy now suffer from obesity, hypertension and depression at rates higher than most Americans. This article goes on to reveal that, in the last decade, the use of antidepressants among pastors and Christian leaders has risen, while the life expectancy among Christian leaders has fallen.[4]

Could it be that this barrage of expectations – and the criticism that so often accompanies them – is *one* of the main reasons (although admittedly not the only one) that so many leaders are leaving the ministry at such alarming rates?

DISAPPOINTMENT IN DEALING WITH PEOPLE

In addition to expectations and criticism, the third source that can do damage to our soul is the inevitable disappointment in dealing with people. Even as I write this chapter, I am once again experiencing disappointment with a group of people in the congregation where I serve. The decision they are making will have negative effect on our congregation, and in the end, I believe it will have a negative effect on them as well. But no matter how hard I try, I can't seem to convince them otherwise.

The disappointment in dealing with people comes in different forms. Some of it comes from the choices people make, or the choices people should make but don't. Some of our disappointment comes from the way a person responds to our leadership, or how a person doesn't respond. As Christian leaders, all of us have known people who we knew were heading down a destructive path, yet somehow we couldn't convince them to take another path and avoid the cliff just ahead.

Some of the disappointments are the result of a person's immaturity, or fickleness, or a reaction from their own brokenness. At other times, it may be the response a person has made in response to a leadership decision we've made. The disappointment may be the result of a legitimate personality difference, or an honest difference of opinion to a new direction we, as a leader, want to take.

I'm not suggesting that the majority of people we deal with are evil or ill-willed toward us. In most cases, that's not the case. Certainly, there are times when a person's response to our leadership is out of a person's stubbornness, or defiance, or ugliness, or sinfulness, or selfishness. But, in all honesty, I don't find this is generally the case. It's not always their fault, and it's not always ours. Sometimes it just "is" – but the disappointment and damage it does to our heart is still real.

What I've found to be the case, after more than thirty-plus years of pastoral ministry, is that it usually doesn't matter what we do or don't do as a leader. In the end, people are going to make their own decisions and do what they want to do. I'm not trying to be negative here. I'm not whining or complaining. I'm just pointing out a reality. And the reality is, as my dad used to say, *"In the end, people are going to do what people are going to do."* So, no matter what the reason, or what the motives may be or may have been, the raw reality is that the disappointments we experience in dealing with people can do damage to our soul.

DISAPPOINTMENT WITH GOD

One of my mentors once wrote, "If you follow Jesus long enough, he will disappoint you." [5] Before you react to that statement, think about it for a moment. As Christian leaders, we've all experienced times when we thought God would certainly come through for us in a situation, and yet seemingly He did not. We've all believed in what we thought were promises from God, but these promises weren't (or have yet to be) fulfilled. We've had times when we desperately needed a breakthrough in an area of our ministry that never came. Or we've fervently prayed for healing for a friend or loved one, yet they died anyway.

I remember recently walking into St. Paul Children's Hospital to visit a courageous eight year old girl who was fighting for her life. Her name was Amara, and she was one of the most joyful, warm winsome little girls I had ever met. She loved butterflies. She loved the color purple. She loved to worship. And, she loved to tell people about Jesus.

Amara had an unexplained condition that had been causing numerous cystic lesions to grow on her brain and spine. She was often in agonizing pain, but remarkably she still possessed a contagious faith that touched many. There was something else uniquely special about Amara; it was as if she sensed her time here on earth would be short. As a result, she had an uncanny closeness to the things of Heaven. She truly was one of the most spiritually sensitive kids I'd ever met. Even her name, Amara, meant "eternal."

As I stood at the foot of her hospital bed, with her parents on one side and my wife on the other, holding Amara's tiny hand, I clearly remember the conflict in my soul. I still feel the pain of it today. The long battle against this medical mystery had been hard fought, but there was nothing else that could be done, Amara needed a miracle. With her favorite worship music playing in the background and tears streaming down our faces, we prayed. In that moment, rumbling around in my head was my theology that God could heal Amara; that God was a good God who wanted to heal her. But my heart was vexed – I feared He might not. It was the classic, "Lord I believe, help my unbelief." We prayed, believing; within the week this precious child passed.

Amara's parents asked me to do the funeral. That was tough.

This isn't an accusation against God or His character (it really isn't), but it's an honest acknowledgement that our journey as Christian leaders leaves us with many mysteries about the ways of God. And, sometimes these disappointments and the accumulation of these mysteries can do damage to our soul. I love God more now and trust Him now more than ever. But, to be truthful to my own journey as a Christian leader, dealing with disappointment with God has done some damage to my soul.

Mix these four ingredients together – expectation, criticism, disappointment in dealing with people, and disappointment with God – add a touch of our own fallen nature, and a big dose of the plans and power of a relentless enemy, and we have a pretty strong concoction that can make our soul pretty sick.

Thankfully, there is a remedy to our soul's sickness, and it's to these core ideas to sustainability in Christian leadership that we now turn.

ACTION AND APPLICATION

Which one of the four sources has most affected your soul? Give examples of each and then describe how these situations have affected your soul.

Expectations:

_____

_____

Criticism:

_____

_____

Disappointment In Dealing With People:

_____

_____

Disappointment With God:

_____

_____

What other sources do you think does damage to a Christian leader's soul?

_____

_____

CHAPTER SIX

IT'S ELEMENTARY MY DEAR WATSON

Come on son, you can do this!
MY DAD

When I was in my 30's pastoring a large and growing congregation, I would frequently come home from a long hard day of work, borrow one of my children's coloring books, sit down at the kitchen table, and start to color. Instead of making decisions about buildings and budgets, I would decide whether the beach ball should be blue or yellow, or whether the umbrella should be red or white. I would experiment with different colors while concentrating on staying within the lines.

Over the years I've found a parallel between my days of coloring and an essential foundation to staying power in Christian leadership. I've discovered that I need to routinely return, like a child, to the elementary idea of "who I am in Christ." I need to put aside all the demands, pressures, and plans that are a part of leading, and remind myself that I am a son, deeply loved and delighted in by the Father. This one practice, probably more than anything else, has been a key – if not *the* key – to building a life of sustainability in ministry.

It's similar to the simple song I grew up singing in Sunday school…

> *Jesus loves me this I know, for the Bible tells me so,*
> *little ones to him belong, they are weak but He is strong.*
> *Yes, Jesus loves me, yes Jesus loves me,*
> *Yes, Jesus loves me, the Bible tells me so.*

I know for some this idea may seem too childlike, but that's the point. Reminding ourselves of who we are, based upon our identity in Christ, is an indispensable foundation for building a life of health and wholeness as a Christian leader.

The late Duke of Windsor tells a story about growing up and being prepared by his father to one day be king. One of the things his father, King George V, regularly said to him was, "My dear boy, you must always remember who you are."[1] For me, when my life as a leader gets crazy and my identity gets confused, I especially need to hear these affirming words from my Father. It's during the difficult days of leading that I must not allow others to define me, but let God remind me who I am. It's when I've "blown it," or when I'm struggling in an area in my life or leadership, that I most need a fresh embrace from the Father.

THE LOVE OF THE FATHER

When I played basketball as a boy, my father always attended my games. He would sit three-quarters of the way up in the bleachers, right behind the players' bench. We lived in a small farming community, so everyone knew everyone in our little town – and they especially knew my dad. Gregarious and outgoing, he was always out and about town, visiting with folks over a cup of coffee at the local diner, or stopping to chat with every person in every aisle as he made his way through the grocery store.

I loved having Dad at my basketball games. It was always so reassuring. Anytime I was uncertain about my performance on the court, I would look over at my coach then glance up into the crowd and find my father's face. He would be clapping, cheering, making recommendations to the coaches or hollering at the refs. He would yell, "Come on Kenny, you can do this!" And that's all I needed. Whether we won or lost, I knew everything would be okay – I had the love and support of my father.

As Christian psychologist David Benner writes,

> Neither knowing God nor knowing self can progress very far unless it begins with a knowledge of how deeply we are loved by God....In order for our knowing of God's love to be truly transformational, it must *become the basis of our identity*. Our identity is who we experience ourselves to be – the "I" each of us carries within. *An identity grounded in God would mean that when we think of who we are, the first thing that would come to mind is our status as someone who is deeply loved by God.* [2]

Revisiting what my Father says about me is similar to a toddler at the park who runs off to play, but routinely runs back to see if Dad is still sitting on the bench watching him. The same is true with us. We need to regularly return to the

Father – not out of duty as a servant, or as a soldier reporting for their next battle assignment, but as a son or daughter deeply loved and delighted in by the Father. This simple practice helps remove the clutter accumulated from leading, calms the clamoring voices in our head, and helps us live and lead from a secure identity found only in the Father.

As Christian leaders, we are very familiar with the biblical idea of our identity being "in Christ." Most of us can readily recite II Corinthians 5:17, *"Therefore, if anyone is in Christ, he is a new creation; the old has gone, the new has come."* We can quickly quote Galatians 2:20, *"I have been crucified with Christ and I no longer live, but Christ lives in me."* And, we can adequately exegete Romans 6: 1-18, Ephesians 4:17–23, Colossians 3: 1-11, and other related "in Him" passages. Knowing the doctrine theologically, however, versus knowing it experientially are two different things. One is a theology spoken behind a podium, the other is a reality experienced during the daily struggles of life and leadership.

My challenge isn't primarily in living out of my identity in Christ, but *continuing* to live out of it! Being applauded and affirmed one moment, and then accused and criticized the next, can certainly create an identity crisis. When the accolades are turning to accusations and my popularity is plummeting, do I know who I am then? When the crowds are dwindling and the critics are circling, is it still well with my soul? During these times, do I still know I'm a son accepted and loved by the Father? That's the question.

Unfortunately our culture – both in the secular and the sacred – doesn't help us much here. In both worlds, we naturally define people according to their popularity, position, or possessions. Author and Pastor Mark Batterson, in his book *Soul Print*, further helps us with this identity issue. He writes,

> The way you see yourself is determined by what you base your identity on. And you have lots of choices. You can base your identity on how you look or who you know. You can base your identity on what you do or how much you make doing it. You can base your identity on titles or degrees. You can base your identity on what you wear or what you drive. There are a million factors that form the composite of our self-concept, but all of us base our identities on something. And what we base our identities on will make us or break us....[3]

In my teens and twenties, I based my identity on my popularity. I was fairly good looking (so they tell me), smart, and athletic. I made the honor roll, was elected class president, selected captain of the basketball team, and dated the prettiest girls in town.

In my thirties, I based my identity on my productivity. I pastored one of the largest and fastest growing congregations in our city. As a result, I became relatively well-known and fairly influential in our city and surrounding region.

In my forties, I based my identity on my position. During that period of my life, I gained most of my security and acquired much of my approval from the reputation of being a "successful" Christian leader.

Now in my fifties, my identity is based primarily on two things: being "in Christ" and being an apprentice of Jesus Christ. Learning to live and lead from my identity found only "in Him" has been one of the greatest – if not the greatest – theological and experiential shifts in my entire life and leadership. I haven't fully arrived, but more than any other time in my life, I can identify with the Apostle Paul when he said, *"I have been crucified with Christ and I no longer live, but Christ lives in me"* (Galatians 2:20).

UNIQUELY YOU

The idea of our identity being "in Christ" doesn't mean we are all clones. Each of us has different temperaments, interests, intellects, talents, passions, and life-experiences. Certainly these traits and experiences make us unique.

Again as Mark Batterson has written,

> There has never been and never will be anyone else like you. But that isn't a testament to you. It's a testament to the God who created you. You are unlike anyone who has ever lived. But that uniqueness isn't a virtue. It's a responsibility. Uniqueness is God's gift to you, and uniqueness is your gift to God. You owe it to yourself to be yourself. But more important, you owe it to the One who designed you and destined you.[4]

Granted, each of us is unique and our individual qualities make us so. But what's critical about our *identity* is to understand that our unique "personality traits" shouldn't become the *only* traits, or the *primary* traits, that define us.

There's nothing wrong with being identified as a person who's witty, or smart, or athletic, or handsome, or strong, or articulate or whatever.... But, what happens to our identity when we are no longer handsome, athletically agile, physically strong, or mentally astute? How do we define ourselves then? How do we define ourselves when others are more attractive, more intelligent, more articulate, or more gifted? Once the unique traits that we've used to define ourselves change – and they inevitably will – who are we then? Who will we need to become next? Trust me, I'm not as handsome as I once was (or at least thought I was). If how I look is what I'm still trying to base my identity on, then it's time to have a full body makeover and get a very extensive and expensive face-lift.

Our unique personality traits can never give us the true and secure identity we need. We've all known the "funny guy" who draws laughs in the lights, but deals with depression in the dark, or the person who appears confident in public, but loathes themselves in private, or the person who seems to "have it all," yet tragically decides to end it all.

Unfortunately, the same is true in Christian circles. How often have we heard about, or known first-hand, a Christian leader who seemed devoted and godly, yet is later revealed as anything but. What causes these discrepancies? Where do these gaps between the exterior and the interior stem from? In many cases there may be chemical, mental, spiritual, or relational dynamics at play. But I think it's safe to say, identity issues – i.e. the question or the confusion around "who am I?" – are also at play.

JESUS AND IDENTITY ISSUES

Even Jesus dealt with this identity issue. In fact many Bible scholars suggest that Satan's temptation of Jesus in the desert was primarily an attack on his identity. These scholars suggest that, with each temptation, Satan was trying to pull Jesus away from his identity found in his Father, and push him toward a false one. Yet Jesus resisted Satan's tactics; He refused his identity to be based upon *power* (turn these stones into bread), or *prestige* (throw yourself off the top of the temple and save yourself so people will know you're the Messiah), or *possessions* (if you bow down and worship me you can have all the kingdoms of the world).[5] Jesus found his identity only in the affirmation and approval of his Father.

Satan's attempt to get Jesus to embrace a false identity wasn't a new trick. He played the same trick on Adam and Eve at the beginning of time, and since that time, he continues to use the same trick on all mankind. It's still the fundamental question – who am I? Where do I find my approval? What do I base my identity on?

What's so ironic about Satan's attack on Jesus' identity is the timeline in which it occurred. The scene right before Satan's temptation of Jesus in the wilderness is the scene of Jesus' baptism by John in the Jordan. One writer paints the picture for us with these words, "In order to understand the temptations of Jesus, we have to understand that Jesus' hair was still wet when he stepped into the desert." [6] As Jesus emerged from the waters of the Jordan his Father declared, "This *is* my beloved son…" With these words the Father affirms the identity of his son. Yet in the very next scene, the first phrase of each temptation that Satan framed was with the counter phrase, "*If* you are the Son of God *then...*" Satan challenged what God had just affirmed.

This is the same thing Satan said to Eve in the garden, "*Has God really said?*" By using this phrase, Satan wasn't only tempting Eve to question God and His motives toward Adam and Eve; he was also tempting Eve to question their very own identity. Were Adam and Eve really who God said they were? Were they really sons and daughters made in His image? Did God really care for them? Would He really provide for them? Could they really trust Him?

Again, Satan's attack was on identity: God's identity, Adam and Eve's identity, and our identity.

Satan's attack didn't work on Jesus, he knew who he was. He knew he was a son loved by the Father. As a result, his ministry and mission flowed from his identity found in his Father.[7] Jesus' ministry didn't define his identity, his identity defined his ministry. *(You may want to read that last sentence again.)*

One Christian leader suggests that after *The Fall* and our subsequent separation from "our Father," we didn't become a planet of apes, as some have proposed. We did, however, become a planet of orphans. Even though God sent his Son to reveal and restore our relationship to God as our Father – could it be that an orphaned world is still man's main sickness? Could it be that our ongoing separation from the God who created us is at the heart of our wanderings and waywardness?

Could it be that many of us, as leaders, aren't living and leading from an identity founded upon and flowing from a father – either an earthly one or more importantly our heavenly one? Could it be that our ministry is defining our identity, instead of our identity defining our ministry? And could it be that a lack of our identity being found in the Father is one of the central reasons for the current crisis in Christian leadership?

I know for some, this summary of the problem may seem too simplistic. But, our identity found "in Christ" and on the love of the Father is an essential foundation for a life of health and wholeness as a leader. Without this foundation being solid, everything else we try to build upon it will be faulty, because nothing else we do in our life or in our leadership can provide the secure foundation found only in the love of the Father. There is no other adequate substitute!

As I've watched over the years, I've seen many leaders lead out of servanthood instead of sonship, or strive through their efforts in ministry to gain something in their soul that only the love of the Father can supply. As I've watched, I've wondered – what percentage of our struggles as leaders stem from our identity issues? How many of the fractures and fault lines found in our lives are formed from an identity not founded on the Father? I would submit that the numbers are larger than we think.

What I've found in my own life, is that when I start striving or pushing too hard or begin leading out of anxiety instead of a place of rest, it's often because I've drifted away from my identity as a son loved by the Father. I've started trying to accomplish things to feed my ego or bolster my insecurity. When I find myself in this state, that's when I need to take a "time-out" and go sit in the lap of the Father for a while.

I haven't resorted to coloring books lately. But, even after all these many years of following Christ and being a leader within the body of Christ, I still regularly, like a child, return to the Father and let him remind me of this simple, elementary truth – I'm a son deeply loved and delighted in by the Father.

ACTION AND APPLICATION

What has been your theological training and Church tradition on the doctrine of your "identity in Christ?"

Strong _____ Weak _____ Average _____

What has been your experience in living out of your "identity found only in Christ?"

_____

_____

Have you had positive or negative father role(s) in your life? How has this affected your life and leadership?

_____

_____

Do you live and lead more as a servant or as a son/daughter?

_____

Do you have a "spiritual father/mother" in your life?

_____

RECOMMENDED RESOURCES:

• *Surrender to Love* by David G. Benner
• *The Marvelous Exchange* by Dick Flaten
• *Experiencing Father's Embrace* by Jack Frost
• *The Return of the Prodigal Son* by Henri Nouwen

CHAPTER SEVEN

CALLING ALL SEA CAPTAINS

The call of God is like the call of the sea;
no one hears it but the one who has the nature of the sea in him.

OSWALD CHAMBERS

A second core idea to sustainability in leadership is routinely revisiting our call into Christian ministry.

Mine was November 24th, 1973.

It was Thanksgiving weekend, and more than 3000 teenagers from across the state of Tennessee had descended upon downtown Nashville. The last night of our denomination's annual youth convention was convening, and I was sitting with some buddies in the upper deck of the War Memorial Auditorium. I don't remember much about the evening, except that the speaker was a popular TV evangelist who was well-known for his inspirational music and firebrand preaching. I don't remember any of the songs we sang, or what the preacher thundered on about that night. What I do remember is that at the end of the service, I made my way from the upper deck, to the front of the stage, and surrendered my life to the call of Christ, only three days before my seventeenth birthday.

My response that evening wasn't an unfounded or uninformed one. Even as a young boy, I had felt a stirring toward the ministry. As a teenager, doing ministry in my Dad's church seemed to further indicate a call of God on my life. Many other events along the way had pointed to the same.

One of the earliest indicators of my call into ministry was when I was seven. It was a Sunday night in my dad's little church in Savannah, Tennessee. The service had ended and people were milling about. Dad was standing in front of the altar and I was standing next to him when a woman by the name of Sister Simms walked up to us. My parents remember her as a godly and devoted intercessor. As a seven year old boy, I remember Sister Simms as an old lady who wore her hair up in a big bun. Sometimes she would get so ecstatic during worship, that her head would start shaking violently. And my concern was that the bun might come loose, letting her long white hair fall down and immodestly dangle down her back. I'm thankful to report that, with the help of 103 well hidden bobby pins, that never happened.

I'm not sure what the conversation with Sister Simms and my dad was about that evening, but I do remember right in the middle of the conversation Sister Simms suddenly got quiet. She closed her eyes, tilted her head up, cocked it to one side, put her hand on my head and in an amplified voice declared, "You have four sons, this one will be one of the preachers in the family." Even though that prophesy was spoken over me more than fifty years ago, every time I reflect on it, I still feel its power and the profound impact it's had on my life.

We all need moments that mark us *for* ministry. And for me, that was one of them.

My dad's call into ministry was also marked at a specific time and a specific place.

Dad was born and raised in a devout Christian home in the back hills of the Ozark Mountains. Like many, when my father became a teenager, he drifted away from his spiritual moorings and wandered in the wilderness for a while. In his early 30's, married and a father of five, Dad returned to God and reconnected with the Church. He was a musician, and *it was the 60's*, so on many Sunday nights my father would travel with a gospel quartet and sing in churches around the area.

As Dad tells the story, the quartet would show up at the church prepared to sing, and then the pastor would ask, "Hey, so who's going to preach tonight?" Not aware that this was part of the gig, the guys would look at each other and point to my dad. On many occasions, Dad would not only be the piano player and lead singer, he became the preacher for the night. These experiences with his singing buddies, along with his increased involvement in our home church, got him wondering whether he should go into Christian ministry fulltime or not.

At the time, Dad worked second shift on an assembly line at Clarke Equipment Company, in Buchanan Michigan. When the shift ended at eleven, he would jump into his brown Studebacker truck and drive the 20 miles home. Once home, his nightly ritual was to get cleaned up, eat some supper, sit down at our old upright piano and begin to sing. The words and melodies from songs like "The Old Rugged Cross," "Draw Me Nearer," and "He Touched Me," would float through the walls, and like a beautiful butterfly, land on my ears. Many nights I would fall asleep hearing my dad singing...

Precious Lord, take my hand, lead me on, let me stand,
I am tired, I am weak, I am worn. Through the storms,
through the night, lead me on to the light, take my hand,
precious Lord, lead me on...

Or words like...

Draw me nearer, nearer precious Lord, to the cross where
Thou hast died...
Draw me nearer, nearer blessed Lord, to Thy precious
bleeding side.

And then ...

He touched me, Oh He Touched me, And Oh the Joy that
floods my soul.
Something, happened and now I know, He touched me and
made me whole.

I was only five, but those experiences still mark me today. Many of the words are faint now, but they still echo through my head and run deep through my heart.

My dad had a good job. With six growing children to feed and clothe, the question of whether to go into ministry fulltime wasn't an easy one. He really struggled with it. Every Sunday morning, he would go to the altar and "seek the Lord" about whether he should or shouldn't. Every night during the week, he would sit down at the piano and do the same. This back and forth struggle got so annoying to my mom, who doesn't say much but when she does her words carry a lot of weight, finally said, "Now Eugene, I want you to either go into the ministry fulltime or hush up about it!"

So Dad finally "heard from the Lord," or was it that the Lord spoke through my mom?! Well, however you interpret it, within a year my dad quit his blue-collar job, sold our little house in Michigan, paid off our debts, loaded us and all of our stuff into a truck, and drove us six hundred miles south to his first pastorate. A little Assemblies of God church in Savannah, Tennessee, Dad's new church had eighteen people in it and promised to pay him $50 a week – *if* it came in the offering. That was May of 1964. Every Sunday, now in his eighties, Dad still drives twenty miles down the road to a little country church that he pastors, and preaches with passion and power.

THE CALL

With the challenges involved in leading, I believe every Christian leader needs to be able to point to a time and a place where God put his finger on their soul and marked them for ministry. The clarity of our call is imperative, because in the end, nothing else will sustain us.

The late W.A. Criswell, at one time one of America's greatest pastors, once wrote, "The first and foremost of all the inward strengths of the pastor is the conviction, deep as life itself, that God has called him into the ministry. If this persuasion is unshakeable, all other elements of the pastor's life will fall into beautiful order and place." [1] As another Christian leader has written, "The work of the ministry is too demanding and difficult for a man to enter it without a sense of divine calling. Men enter and then leave ministry usually because they lack a sense of divine urgency. Nothing less than a definite call from God could ever give a man success in the ministry." [2]

As both of these writers so emphatically state, being involved in Christian ministry must be initiated and sustained by a divine call. A call to Christian ministry must be more than the end product of an educational process, or our response to the urgings of family or friends. It must be more than a noble idea, and it certainly must be more than a convenient career choice. A clear call by God must be, and ultimately should be, the only reason we are serving as leaders in God's church. Charles Bridges, in his classic work *The Christian Ministry,* reinforces this same idea with these pointed words. "We may sometimes trace Ministerial failure *to the very threshold of the entrance to the work*. Was the call to the sacred office clear in the order of the church, and according to the will of God?" [3]

Even the Apostle Paul understood the importance of regularly revisiting his call. Here's a man who penned over a third of the New Testament, planted churches throughout Asia Minor, received special revelation from God, and was given a special assignment from God. One would think that Paul was always strong, always certain, always courageous, always confident – but the scripture indicates otherwise. Paul experienced the expectations and accusations of others. He also battled with his own insecurities and uncertainties. Paul had his critics. He had his congregational coups. He had his friends who betrayed him and his coworkers who deserted him. He had his doubts, fears, harassments and hardships. [4]

Yet, in in the midst of these difficulties and uncertainties, it was the clarity of his call and his commitment to that call that brought focus and fortitude to his life and leadership. The following are a few of the many references Paul made concerning his call into ministry:

- "Paul, a servant of Christ Jesus, called to be an apostle and set apart for the gospel of God…" Romans 1:1
- "Through him and for his name sake, we received grace and apostleship to call people from among all the Gentiles to have obedience that comes from faith." Romans 1:5
- "So then, men ought to regard us as servants of Christ and as those entrusted with the secret things of God." I Corinthians 4:1
- "Even though I may not be an apostle to others, surely I am to you! For you are the seal of my apostleship in the Lord." I Corinthians 9:2
- "But when God, who set me apart from birth and called me by his grace, was pleased to reveal his Son in me so that I might preach him among the Gentiles…" Galatians 1:15,16
- "I became a servant of this gospel by the gift of God's grace…" Ephesians 3:7

- "Paul, an apostle of Christ Jesus, by the will of God..." Colossians 1:1
- "I have become its servant (the Church) by the commission God gave me to present to you the word of God in its fullness..." Colossians 1: 25
- "I thank Christ Jesus our Lord, who has given me strength, that he considered me faithful appointing me to his service." I Timothy 1:12

Just reading these few verses about Paul's call into ministry strengthens me in mine!

I must confess, my biggest temptation as a Christian minister isn't watching porn, or skimming funds, or running off with the organ player (we don't have an organ!). My biggest temptation is self-pity. When things in ministry aren't going the way I want, or the way I think they should, that's when I find that faith and fortitude seem to easily leak out of my heart. When that happens, I start whining. I want to check out. I start feeling sorry for myself. I start having a good "oh woe is me" pity party.

If the Apostle Paul experienced the ups and downs of ministry, what makes me think I won't? If he had friends who betrayed him and coworkers who deserted him, why do I think it should be any different for me? If Paul had his critics why do I think I won't have mine? If Paul dealt with harassments and hardships why do I think I should be exempt?

In the same way Paul found his footing and strengthened his resolve in Christian ministry by revisiting his call – you and I must do the same.

THE SPECIFICS OF OUR CALL

I had only met the man the day before, but the question he was about to ask me would change my entire approach to Christian leadership.

The church I was pastoring was going through major turmoil. We needed to make some changes but weren't sure which changes to make. So a member of our congregation recommended we bring a consultant in to help us figure some things out.

The first day, the consultant spent several hours with me alone, followed by individual time with each staff member and then we finished the long day by meeting as a team. The following morning, I met with the consultant again privately, and that's when he asked me a question that would set in motion a whole new way of thinking about my role as a pastor and Christian leader.

Sitting across from me at the large conference table the consultant said, "Pastor Ken, as you and your team are assessing some things that need to be changed around here, and as you are considering the next season of your own role within your congregation, here's my question to you. Do you want to be your church's CEO or its shepherd?"

I didn't know what to say. I'm sure my blank stare and long silence probably said it all. I had no idea what he meant. I cleared my throat, projected the best self-confident leadership façade I could, and sheepishly asked, "So, uh, what do you mean CEO or shepherd?" "Well," he replied, "you can continue being the primary person who casts the vision, plans the strategy, manages the staff, oversees the organizational systems, chairs the board meetings and the staff meetings and the budget meetings and the building meetings, or you can become the person whose primary responsibility is to set the spiritual tone of your congregation, nurture the spiritual life of your staff and key leaders, and provide care for the souls of those you serve."

I still didn't fully understand what he meant, but it was starting to sink in and starting to make some sense. In an attempt to soften the blow to my ego and reassure me a bit, the consultant continued, "It's not a question of whether you are gifted enough to do both, the reality is, you don't have the time, or the energy, or the focus, to do both and to do either one of them adequately. And in this particular season of your life as a leader, you need to decide which one it will be."

That conversation challenged me to reconsider what *my* specific call from God was and what *my* specific role within His Church should be. That was in 2006, and since then I've been on a journey thinking about and approaching the role of a leader *and* the mission of the Church in a whole new way.

CONFUSION ABOUT OUR CALL

The longer I'm in ministry, and the more interaction I have with other pastors and Christian leaders, the more I'm convinced there's a lot of confusion over the purpose of the Church and the role of God's leaders within it. I do understand, and I do agree that every Christian leader has different ministry gifts. I do acknowledge that the title "pastor" is often used as a generic catch-all role. But, I'm still convinced that we need to return to a biblical definition of the purpose of the church and the pastor and Christian leader's specific role within God's church.

I'm not suggesting that every "pastor" has to be a shepherd; some are called and gifted as teachers, evangelists, or prophets. Granted, some have more "leadership gifts" than others. Some have gifts of helps and some have gifts of mercy. Some have the gift of administration, while some don't! There is a large diversity of gift-mixes needed under the umbrella of "pastoring." But my appeal, and my point, is that we need to revisit *our* specific call and *our* specific role that God has assigned for *us* within His church. The Apostle Paul was clear about his call into Christian service, and he was also clear on the *specifics* of his call. We must be clear as well.

Eugene Peterson in his masterful book, *The Contemplative Pastor*, makes the case that "the essence of being a pastor begs for redefinition," [5] he then goes on to define what he believes that redefinition is – or at least should be. He writes:

> A Reformation may be in process in the way pastors do their work. It may turn out to be as significant as the theological reformation of the sixteenth century… The vocational reformation of our time (if it turns out to be that) is a rediscovery of the pastoral work of the cure of souls.
>
> I am not the only pastor who has discovered this old identity. More and more pastors are embracing this way of pastoral work and are finding themselves authenticated by it. There are not a lot of us. We are by no means a majority, not even a high-profile minority. But one by one, pastors are rejecting the job description that has been handed to them and are taking on

this new one or, as it turns out, the old one that has been in use for most of the Christian centuries.

This is the pastoral work that is historically termed the cure of soul. The primary sense of *cura* in Latin is "care," with undertones of "cure." The cure of souls, then, is the Scripture-directed, prayer-shaped care that is devoted to persons singly or in groups, in settings sacred and profane. *It is a determination to work at the center, to concentrate on the essential.* [6]

Peterson goes on to contrast the pastoral ministry of "cure of souls" with what it has more commonly become, what he calls "running a church." The contrast between the two doesn't mean that the organizational duties of "running a church" aren't needed. It's a question concerning which role gets the most attention and which role is producing what. *As shepherds, are we helping people grow into authentic followers of Jesus Christ, or as CEOs, are we working to attract more consumers so we can dispense more Christian programs and products?*

My point in using Peterson's extended quote is to encourage us to reconsider the role of a shepherd within the mission of the Church. I would contend that we desperately need to return to the exercise of authentic spiritual leadership and the needed role of pastoral ministry, not simply as culturally defined, but as biblically defined. This is actually the same question the apostles were asking in Acts 6: *"What is our role as spiritual leaders within the church and in light of that role, how do we serve the administrative roles that are not primary but are still necessary?"* The same question goes back to Paul's instruction in Ephesians 4: 1 – 16, where Paul explains that there are different gifts given for different roles within God's Church.

I'm not arguing that we should neglect skillful leadership and organizational effectiveness for the sake of the shepherding role in the "cure of souls." What I'm appealing for, however, is a balance between the two. Within much of the church today, the emphasis seems to be more on the role of the CEO, and less on the role of the shepherding of souls. This isn't an "either or" argument but a "both and." We need visionary and apostolic leadership. We need prophets. We need evangelists. We need teachers. We need shepherds. *And* we need the gifts of leadership and administration necessary for "running a church." But, we must not let the organizational elements involved in running a church override the need for a biblically defined pastoral ministry; one that provides oversight, care, nurturing, and the shaping of spiritual souls.

One church leader, who has astutely observed the confusion over leadership roles within the church, offers us two kinds of leadership options to consider. The first option is an approach to ministry that is primarily need-based, man-centered, consumer-driven, and culturally defined. The second option is an approach to ministry that is redemptively centered, God-focused, biblically defined, and scripturally prioritized.[7] Which option we choose determines the role we play, and the outcomes we can expect.

I'm concerned that too many of us have chosen the former over the latter, and as a result we are trying to keep up with what the culture demands of us, instead of doing what the scripture defines for us. There were several years in my minis-try where I became a pretty good CEO, but a rather neglectful shepherd in the caring of souls. Regrettably, both I and the congregation I served at the time, paid the price.

The consultant that day had no idea the question he posed to me would redirect my entire approach to Christian lead-ership. I'm grateful to say, my life and leadership is healthier because of it. I believe those I currently serve would say the same thing about the health of their own spiritual souls.

Routinely revisiting our call into ministry, and being clear about the specifics of our call, is a core idea to building a life of sustainability in Christian leadership.

ACTION AND APPLICATION

Is there a specific time and place where God called you into the ministry? If so describe the event.

_____

_____

Do you feel you are clear regarding the *specifics* of your call? If so, list your different gifts and the specific call you believe God has assigned to you in the body of Christ.

_____

_____

RECOMMENDED APPLICATIONS:

List several verses in the bible that have to do with your call into ministry and review them regularly.

If you had a specific call into ministry, revisit it in your mind and spirit, and let it encourage and strengthen your heart.

Review your current job description/ministry responsibilities and consider how much of what you are doing is in alignment with what you believe are the specifics of your call. Is it 20% 50% 70% or ___ %?

RECOMMENDED RESOURCES:

- *Spiritual Leadership* by Dr. Henry and Dr. Richard Blackaby
- *Pastoral Ministry* by John McArthur Jr.
- *Am I Called? The Summons To Pastoral Ministry* by Dave Harvey

CHAPTER EIGHT

A FEW MORE SILENT PREACHERS

Only when we have learned to be truly silent are we able to speak the word that is needed when it is needed.

RICHARD FOSTER

On a summer morning well before sunrise, I found myself trudging through the Tennessee woods to go squirrel hunting with my dad and older brother, David. We settled beneath an oak tree and waited for unsuspecting squirrels to show up. I sat with my back against the trunk of the tree, my 4-10 shotgun lying across my lap, swatting at an army of incoming kamikaze mosquitos. I was groggy from getting up so early, and being an eleven year old kid, it didn't take me long to get bored and start fidgeting. I began kicking at the acorns lying at my feet and thought, "It seems a shame to let all that ammo go to waste!" So I picked up a handful, and starting throwing them at the trees across the creek. And that's when in mid-throw, Dad whispered, "Now son, if the squirrels are going to come out, you've gotta be quiet and stay still."

There are many tools to help build a life of staying power in the life of a Christian leader but the two that I believe are most essential, and probably the most overlooked, are the spiritual disciplines of solitude and silence. Self-awareness is the third core idea to greater sustainability in Christian leadership, and nothing helps us to be personally more mindful and self-aware than practicing times of solitude and silence.

Throughout the centuries, the men and women who've given the most attention to their inner life have regularly engaged in these two spiritual disciplines. Jesus did. John the Baptist, St. Francis of Assisi, Teresa of Avila, Thomas à Kempis, Dietrich Bonhoeffer, Mother Teresa, Thomas Merton, Henri Nouwen, A.W. Tozer, and a host of other Christian leaders throughout the centuries did, and some continue to do so today.

One source defines the spiritual discipline of solitude as:

- *The creation of an open, empty space in our lives by purposefully abstaining from interaction with other human beings, so that, freed from competing loyalties, we can be found by God.* [1]

The same source defines the spiritual discipline of silence as:

- *Closing off our souls from "sounds," whether noise, or music, or words, so that we may better still the inner chatter and clatter of our noisy hearts and be increasingly attentive to God.* [2]

Although these two definitions are certainly helpful, our challenge hasn't been so much in defining them, but in *practicing* them. In a world as noisy and hurried as ours, being quiet and staying still for any length of time is similar to my squirrel hunting experience as an eleven year old boy. It's rather difficult to do.

What I've discovered, as have many others, is that to develop a life of sustainability in ministry, extended times of solitude and silence are essential. One leader considered these two practices so essential that he believed, "without [them] it is impossible to live a spiritual life." [3] And another leader suggested that "solitude is the most radical of the disciplines for life in the spirit." [4] If these two quotes aren't convincing enough, consider this Christian leader's astonishing confession. She writes, "...my journey into solitude and silence has been the *single most meaningful* aspect of my spiritual life to date – a pretty strong statement for one who has been a Christian since she was four years old!" [5]

But why is this? Why is solitude and silence so central to building a life of staying power in Christian ministry? Several reasons could be given, but let me offer four primary ones.

OUR SOUL COMES OUT OF HIDING

First, it's in solitude and silence that our soul comes out of hiding.

As the writer Parker Palmer so succinctly describes, our soul is like a wild animal, and if you want it to come out of hiding, you must sit in silence and wait. He writes:

The soul is like a wild animal – tough, resilient, re-sourceful, savvy, self-sufficient. It knows how to survive in hard places. But it is also shy. Just like a wild animal it seeks safety in the underbrush. If we want to see a wild animal, we know that the last thing we should do is go crashing through the woods yelling for it to come out. But if we will walk quietly into the woods, sit patiently by the base of the tree, and fade into the surroundings, the wild animal we seek might put in an appearance. [6]

As Palmer describes it, since hiding is the way of the soul, then extended times of solitude and silence are necessary for our soul to come out and show itself. As we engage in these two disciplines, our pain, confusion, wounds, questions, long-ings, disappointments, dreams – and whatever else may be hiding there – can safely surface. If we'll wait long enough, some of the idols of our soul are sure to emerge. If we'll slow down long enough, some of our false lovers will certainly show up. If we'll be quiet and stay still, the longings of our soul that were once passionate and prominent but are now lying dormant under duty and disappointments, will once again stir and start to speak.

Ruth Haley Barton further helps us understand this connection between engaging in solitude and silence and uncovering the true state of our soul, with these words.

The longing for solitude is ... the longing to find ourselves, to be in touch with what is *most real within us*, that which is more solid and enduring *than what defines us externally.* But it's tricky to get the soul to come out...We are not very safe for ourselves, because our internal experience involves continual critique and judgment, and the tender soul does not want to risk it. *Unfortunately, a lot of our religious activity is very noisy as well;* oftentimes we're just an organized group of people crashing through the woods together, making so much noise that there's no soul in sight... There are very few places where the soul is truly safe, where the knowing, the questions, the longings of the soul are welcomed, received and listen to rather than evaluated, judged or beaten out of us. [7]

Certainly, we live in a noisy world. Phones ringing. People talking. Children playing. Cars passing. Trucks rumbling. Horns honking. Planes humming. Machines clanking. Music booming. T.V.s blaring. Neighbors yelling. Dogs barking. Siblings squabbling. Babies crying. For most of us, constant noise is a common companion, and whether we're aware of it or not, it has an effect on us.

In fact, studies show that constant noise not only pollutes our environment, but it's also detrimental to our health. Annoyance, agitation, aggression, mood swings, sleep disturbances, hypertension, and high stress levels – can be linked, either partially or directly, to increased levels of incessant noise. [8]

It's not only the constant noise in our outer world that affects us, but it's also the endless chatter in our inner world that takes its toll. Researchers tell us that on average a person has about 90,000 thoughts a day. These thoughts are responses to both what's happening outside of our head as well as what's happening inside our head.

For example, right now I'm hearing my neighbor's dog barking, while my mind is reminding me of that important phone call that I have to make, and at the same time that little voice in my head is telling me I'll never get this book finished. When we add the ongoing self-talk rumbling around in our head to the external and internal noises already in our head, well that makes what's happening between our ears a very noisy place!

What I've found, is that when I take the time to silence the noise of my outer world and turn down the chatter of my inner world, I eventually begin to more clearly hear, more accurately see, and more intensely feel what is *truly* happening in my soul. That's why practicing solitude and silence is so essential for anyone who wants to cultivate greater self-awareness and move toward a life of greater inner health and wholeness.

THE LOVER OF OUR SOUL SHOWS UP TO SPEAK

There's a second benefit to practicing solitude and silence. It's in solitude and silence where the Lover of our soul shows up to speak.

My wife and I have friends who own a King Charles spaniel named Caycee. Now I'm not an animal psychologist but just from observation I am convinced this dog has issues. I think she has a severe case of ADHD. During dinner, the dog at some point invariably comes running into the room in a frenzied state, legs flailing, slip sliding across the wood floor. The first time we experienced this strange behavior, we had no idea what was going on. After seeing her crazy antics a few more times, we finally figured it out. Caycee becomes crazed whenever a light reflection invades her doggy domain. Whether it's a reflection shining on the wall, or a small light bouncing off the ceiling, Casey will run into the room barking, and like a motorized merry-go-round, start spinning in circles.

Many of us are a bit like Casey. We have the tendency to chase shiny objects and spin in circles. We hurry here and hurry there. Run off to this meeting and then scurry over to that one. Rush off to one activity and dart over to another one. We get home late, get up early and then rush off at a frenzied pace repeating the same insane cycle.

It's interesting and insightful that the Swahili word for "white man" (i.e. westerner) – is *mazungu* – which literally means "one who spins around." What an apt description of many of us who live in a modernized, westernized world. We seem to be going fast in every direction, but in reality, are we really going anywhere at all? We run in endless circles, making ourselves dizzy and frequently making ourselves sick. [9]

We're not only a hurried society; like Casey, we're also a distracted one. We're distracted for many reasons. One of the main reasons is the endless options available to us. Whether its toothpaste, soap, shampoo, cell phones, sporting gear, cereal, ice cream, or the gazillion items at our favorite buffet – about anything and everything is available to us. Whether it's offered at the nearest mall, our warehouse super store, a 24/7 shopping network, or by the click of a button – we are inundated and often overwhelmed with endless options.

The same is true of our entertainment. Do we really need

access to movies, music, news, weather, sports, cooking, stocks, and home decorating – 24 hours a day, seven days a week? Do we really need six T.V. shows running simultaneously on a 72 inch HD T.V. screen? Do we really need an app for everything? Over five hundred years ago, the French philosopher Blaise Pascal made this insightful and prophetic observation, "By means of a diversion, we can avoid our own company twenty-four hours a day." [10] It seems we are living in that day.

Whatever the item is, or wherever it's offered, we're flooded with options. With each option a choice is required, and with each choice our ADHD increases. Should I go here or go there? Should I buy this or buy that? Should I wear this or wear that? It's like dropping a medieval monk into the middle of Times Square – the stimulus is overwhelming.

Chasing more bright lights or adding more activities to our already haggard and margin-less lives clearly isn't the remedy. Could it be that we are chasing after a way of life we think we want, yet looking for it in all the wrong places?

One modern day monk, while visiting the U.S. from Europe, made this observation about our hurried and distracted culture. He writes:

> What most strikes me, being back in the United States, is the full force of the restlessness, the loneliness, and the tension that holds so many people. The conversations I had today were about spiritual survival. So many of my friends feel overwhelmed by the many demands made on them; few feel the inner peace and joy they so much desire…There seems to be a moun-

tain of obstacles preventing people from being *where their hearts want to be...* The astonishing thing is that the battle for survival has become so 'normal' that few people really believe that it can be different....[11]

But life doesn't have to be this way. The bible promises us another way to live.

- In Psalms, David tells us that "only in God is our soul at rest" (Psalms 62:1).
- Isaiah the prophet promises that, "those who wait upon the Lord shall renew their strength" (Isaiah 40:31).
- Jesus said, "Come to me all you who are weary and heavy laden and I will give you rest" (Matthew 11:28).
- Psalms 91:1 says, "Those who dwell in the shelter of the Most High will rest in the shadow of the almighty."
- Psalms 16:8 states, "I will keep my eyes always on the Lord. With him at my right hand I will not be shaken."
- Hebrews 4:9 says, "There remains therefore a rest for the people of God."

These verses, and many others, offer a prescription to a way of life that doesn't have to be dominated by hurry and distraction. But, in an age as sophisticated as ours, do we believe these ancient instructions are real remedies for our modern times? Do we believe that solitude and silence can bring healing to our hectic and hurried souls? It's a question, we as Christian leaders, need to ask and honestly answer; not only for ourselves, but for those we lead and for those we serve.

In a world as hurried and distracted as ours, all of us periodically lose our way. So it's extremely important to routinely be still and silent. We need to assess how the pressure from ministry is shaping us, and where the pace of life and leadership is pushing us. Like a raft on open seas, drifting is often dangerous, and like a diver in deep water, prolonged pressure is detrimental. Therefore, regularly taking the time to stop and find out where we're going, and who we are becoming, is a very, very wise thing to do.

Granted, God can get our attention and speak to us at any time (and sometimes He does). And admittedly, we need to learn to have ongoing conversations with God in the everyday activities of life (and there is a way to do that). God seldom forces himself on us. Instead, like a lover waiting to be with the one he loves – God patiently waits. I find it ironic that the only One who can provide the kind of life we say we want is often the very One we push to the side as we hurry by. We chase after things we think we want, yet being with God is what we desperately need. Just one word from Him can redirect our path. Just one glimpse can rekindle our heart. Just one touch can refresh our soul.

A LIFE OF SUBSTANCE IS SHAPED

There's a third benefit to solitude and silence.

It's in solitude and silence where a life of substance is most profoundly shaped.

Thomas Merton asserts that the substance of a man isn't forged while mingling with the muddled masses but in the reflective moments of solitude and silence. He writes, "The great temptation of modern man is not physical solitude but immersion in the mass of other men...*There is actually no more dangerous solitude than that of the man who is lost in a crowd*....Very often it is the solitary who has the most to say; not that he uses many words, but what he says is new, substantial, unique...*He has something real to give because he himself is real.*" [12]

Dietrich Bonhoeffer in his classic work, *Life Together*, makes a similar observation when he writes, "Let him who cannot be alone beware of community. ...One who wants fellowship without solitude plunges into the void of words and feelings...." [13] The point Bonhoeffer makes is that the person who doesn't know who they are when alone will attempt to find their identity, or hide from their real identity, by being emerged in the masses.

All the great men and women throughout the history of the Church have understood this principle: lives of substance are most profoundly shaped during seasons of solitude and silence. Moses. Elijah. Jeremiah. John the Baptist. Jesus. St. Francis of Assisi. St. John of the Cross. George Mueller. Hudson Taylor. Frank Laubach. Amy Carmichael. Dietrich Bonhoeffer. Brother Lawrence...and the list goes on.

In fact, studies on the developmental stages in the life of a Christian leader confirm this pattern: lives of substance are shaped in solitude and silence. Sometimes these seasons are called the dark night of the soul, or a prolonged period of God's silence, or a desert experience. These seasons can come about for different reasons. They can occur because of a personal crisis, a protracted illness, or a providential circumstance in the life of a leader. They may be the result of some disciplinary action that's forced a leader to step out of ministry for an extended season; just the opposite, a leader by his own initiative may remove himself from ministry for the purpose of personal renewal or a time of retooling. Whatever these seasons are called, and for whatever reasons they may have come about – extended times of silence and solitude are essential for shaping a life of substance in the life of a leader. [14]

One of my colleagues described it this way, "The desert is often the place where God sends His children He is most pleased with." Wow! Yes, for many leaders the desert can become a friend and not a foe, because it's there – in times of solitude and silence that God most profoundly shapes our lives into a life of deeper substance.

SOMETHING OF SUBSTANCE TO SAY

Lastly, there's a fourth benefit.

It's in silence and solitude where leaders develop lives of deeper substance, but it's also the place where leaders develop lives with something of substance to say.

We live in a time when fewer words in the church would do us all some good. Fewer sermons and a few more lives of substance with something of significance to say would be really refreshing. The truth is, many Christian leaders are only echoing what everyone else is saying, or repeating what has already been said. We need fewer pulpiteers and a few more prophets.

We need a few less entertainers and a few more proclaimers. We need some fresh voices.

A.W. Tozer, one of the great prophetic voices of the twentieth century, put it this way, "Between the scribe who has read and the prophet who has seen [and heard] there is a difference as wide as the sea. We are today overrun with orthodox scribes, but the prophets, where are they? The hard voice of the scribe sounds over evangelicalism, but the Church waits for the tender voice of the saint who has penetrated the veil and has gazed with inward eye upon the Wonder that is God." Tozer sums up his point with this penetrating line. "The tragedy is that our eternal welfare depends upon our hearing, and we have trained our ears not to hear." [15]

In his wonderful book, *The Rest Of God*, pastor and author Mark Buchanan warns Christian leaders about the subtle danger of people stopping to listen to us, without us first stopping to ask ourselves, *who are we stopping to listen to?* Mark writes, "All of our authority is derived. Either God gives us words, or we are only giving opinions. Either God vouches for us, or our credentials are forged...*Our speaking comes out of our listening. What we say comes out of what we hear.* We have to be people who listen, day and night, to God. Our utterances ought to be as Jesus's were: an echoing of the Father, an imitation of him." [16]

A leader's ability to "hear from the Father" is no small thing. In fact, Robert J. Clinton, perhaps the leading authority on leadership emergence patterns (how a leader develops over time), contends that a spiritual leader's ability to "hear and receive truth from God" is central to a leader's ability to establish and exercise spiritual influence.[17] Dr. Clinton's studies on the life of leaders in the Bible and throughout the history of the Church show that God first teaches emerging leaders how to hear and receive truth for their own lives, which then becomes the stepping stone for that leader's ability to hear and receive truth for those they lead.[18] In reality, without our willingness to stop long enough to listen to God, we really have nothing of substance to say.

Jesus had something of substance to say, and the people of his day recognized he did. In contrast to the religious leaders who droned on and on about the already well-known and worn-out debates of the Torah, the people recognized Jesus as a fresh voice, a prophet with something of substance to say. Matthew records it this way. "When Jesus had finished saying these things (i.e. the teaching of the Sermon on the Mount), the crowds were amazed at his teaching, because he taught as one who had authority, and not as their teachers of the law" (Matthew 7: 28 & 29).

Why was that? Why did Jesus speak as one with authority? Let me offer two primary reasons. First, Jesus regularly spent time in solitude and silence so he could *hear* what His Father was saying and *see* what His Father was doing. And second, Jesus not only looked and listened to the Father but he *obeyed* what he heard and *did* what he saw.[19] In essence, there was perfect harmony between who Jesus was and what Jesus said. His life matched his words and his words matched his life. Jesus' authenticity produced his authority.

This authenticity to authority principle is a universal one. For example, I prefer working with a fitness trainer who's *in* shape opposed to one's who's not. I believe it's best to get marriage counseling from someone who has a good marriage versus someone who doesn't. And I think it's wisest to learn how to make a million dollars from someone who's made a million instead of someone who's only read the brochure and gone to the seminar.

The same authenticity to authority principle holds true for us as Christian leaders. Teaching on tithing when I'm not, has little authority. Talking about holiness when I'm not living it (or at least trying to), is hollow and hypocritical. In fact, this ratio of authenticity to authority is why the Bible says more about what a spiritual leader is *to be* than what a spiritual leader is *to do*. Phillips Brooks, a prominent clergyman during the nineteenth century, put it this way, "What the minister *is* is far more important than what he is able to do, for what he *is* gives force to what he *does*. In the long run, ministry is what we *are* as much as what we *do*." [20]

I know a pastor who traveled extensively around the country speaking at marriage and family conferences. He was a great communicator and had excellent material on the topic. Standing ovations at the end of his sessions weren't uncommon. But it was later learned that in several cities where he routinely traveled to speak, the woman who ended up in his bed at night, quite often wasn't his wife. The material he was communicating was true, but the life he was living wasn't. When our authenticity is compromised, so is our authority.

Granted, none of us are perfect. We all have our faults and failures. But, when a gap is growing between what we say and what we do, then, in all honestly we have nothing of substance to say and we would be wise to stop talking. What's happening below the waterline of our life really is the most important thing about us. And practicing the disciplines of solitude and silence – perhaps more than any of the other spiritual disciplines – will help us shape a life of greater substance, so when we do emerge from these seasons we'll have something of substance to say.

I want to be clear: by focusing on solitude and silence I'm not down playing the importance of other spiritual disciplines. Prayer, worship, fasting, the study, memorization and meditation of God's word, and other spiritual practices are all central to building a life of substance. But I would suggest that without taking the time to be still and silent, and letting the truth of God's Word go deep and reveal the true state of our soul, we can become just professional handlers of God's Word. As we all know, that's a dangerous deception. We must allow the substantive and transformational work of God's Word do its work in our own lives first, and then offer it to those we serve.

As we close this chapter let me make one disclaimer. You don't have to be a monk or modern day mystic to practice solitude and silence. Indeed, it may take more effort for an action-oriented extrovert than it does a contemplative-introvert. However, wherever we fall on the temperament scale, practicing this discipline can be done and needs to be done. And, if you are a type A personality it's probably even more important that you learn to slow down and practice greater self-awareness.

Solitude and silence is essential for a life of staying power in the life of every leader. Whether it's short blocks of time weekly, extended times quarterly, or more extended times yearly, it's imperative that we are routinely finding the time to let our soul come out of hiding, and the Lover of our soul show up to speak. This will result in a life of substance and have something of greater substance to say.

I don't squirrel hunt anymore, but I still frequently hear my Father say, "Now son, you need to be quiet and stay still for a while."

ACTION AND APPLICATION

Do you regularly practice solitude and silence?

_____

_____

What other spiritual disciplines help you get in touch with the true state of your soul?

_____

_____

What are other ways God "speaks to you?"

_____

_____

Are there any growing gaps in your life between your authenticity and your authority?

_____

_____

RECOMMENDED RESOURCES:
- *Solitude and Silence* by Ruth Haley Barton
- *Sacred Rhythms* by Ruth Haley Barton
- *Overcoming The Dark Side Of Leadership* by Gary L. McIntosh and Samuel D. Rima

CHAPTER NINE

TWISTED OR TRANSFORMED?

*The best thing you can bring to your leadership
is your own transforming self.*

RUTH HALEY BARTON

Tuesday, March 9, 2004 started out like any other day. I awoke at 6:30, headed downstairs, put on the coffee, and waited for my wife to join me in the kitchen. We poured our coffees and moved into the living room to begin our morning routine. Our conversation drifted to our kids, our responsibilities at work, and some thoughts about our future.

Our nineteen-year-old son interrupted our conversation and asked Mom to come into his room to talk. This was very unusual. Being a late night person, he was rarely awake at this time of the morning, much less initiating meaningful conversation. Sitting on the side of his bed, they talked about topics he loved – music, movies, and sports – none of us knew how cherished this brief, unexpected, early morning exchange between my wife and our son would become.

Later, my wife and I went back upstairs to get ready for the day. We exchanged our normal "I love yous," kissed, said our goodbyes, and headed off in opposite directions.

I drove to the health club, and my wife drove our daughter to work. During their short drive, they talked, laughed, and listened to music. After dropping her off, my wife headed to a women's Bible study that she attended every other Tuesday morning. It was just another drive, on another morning, at the start of another day.

I had finished my workout, and was on my way home when my cell phone rang. My daughter, on the other end of the line, calmly said, "Dad, the hospital just called me trying to reach you. They said Mom's been in a car accident. They didn't give me any further details; that's all I know."

I hurried home, picked up my son, and rushed to the emergency room. When we arrived, it was clear the situation was serious. My wife had been hit by a large sports utility vehicle on the driver's side of her car. She was resuscitated at the scene, and now lay unconscious in front of me.

I struggled to believe it. The day had started out like any other, but, without warning, this journey called "life" had taken a sharp, unexpected turn. It would never be the same. Three days later, on March 12th, 2004 at 12:40 p.m., my wife was pronounced dead from the result of a brain trauma. She was only forty-seven years old.

I retell my story here only to make this point: Life shapes us. It's not a matter of *if*, it's only a matter of *how*. Within weeks of my wife's death, it became clear that how I responded to the difficult days ahead would shape me. It wasn't a question of *if* the tragedy would shape me, it was only a question of *how* would it shape me. Would it change me for the better or for the worse? Would it move me towards or away from the person I hoped to become? The answer would be determined by my response. The choice was mine.

Earlier in my life (and certainly in my leadership), my approach during times of difficulty was never, "How should I respond?" My pattern was the exact opposite. I despised difficulties. I ran from setbacks. I avoided suffering. My basic response was to cry and complain, kick and scream, whine and pout. Pity parties were a regularly scheduled event.

Then ten years before my wife's accident, while reading James 1: 2 – 4, I experienced a fundamental shift in my approach toward difficulty. The passage reads, *"Consider it pure joy whenever you face trials of many kinds, because you know that the testing of your faith develops perseverance. Perseverance must finish its work so that you may be mature and complete,"*

Although I had read this passage on many occasions, this time it took hold of me in a different way. I began to embrace it with deeper meaning. I realized that "difficulties will always be part of the journey (it's called 'life'), and, since adversity is unavoidable, I should at least grow from them as I go through them." *This simple insight set in motion a profound change in my life, and eventually in my leadership.*

Over time, my new outlook toward difficulties radically reoriented my mental attitude and dramatically re-wired my emotional responses to these times. Instead of viewing trials as unwanted pain, I now approached them as opportunities for personal growth. Instead of seeing adversity as nothing more than suffering and setback, I now embraced them as an occasion to be shaped more and more into the character of Christ.

I clearly remember the morning this principle, "How will I respond?" took root in my life. It was a few days after my wife's passing, and I was making my bed, when right in the middle of tucking in the sheets, my anger surged. A voice in my head screamed, "I'm a forty-seven-year-old man, starting life all over, making my king-sized bed, alone. I hate this. This isn't fair!"

As I straightened the sheets, arranged the comforter, and fluffed the pillows, the irrepressible thoughts continued, and the anger intensified. Then, like a loose cog clicking into place, it became crystal clear, *"How I respond, even in these moments of seemingly ordinary activities, will determine who I become."* That simple thought was revolutionary. As I made my bed the following weeks, instead of occasions for anger and resentment, these domestic chores became opportunities to practice servanthood and humility, patience and peace, contentment and gratitude.

This new attitude wasn't limited to making my bed. It extended to shopping at the grocery store, washing dishes, paying the bills, and doing laundry. When the little old lady in the express checkout line in front of me, chatted with the cashier about her latest doctor's visit, a recent trip to the casino, and updates on all twenty-nine grandchildren, would I be pleasant and patient, or rude and annoyed? After hitting the golf ball, off the same tee, into the same woods, for the third time, would I be irate, or graciously accept my golfing limitations? When the driver behind me honked within a nanosecond of the red light turning green, how would I respond? (I still have some work to do in this area.) *All of my daily activities became sacred moments for meaningful formation.*

As a way to *practice* Christ-like responses in my daily activities, I began a very unusual ritual. Every morning as I got dressed, I picked up from my nightstand a small spike-like nail, and put it in my pants pocket. The nail served as a tangible reminder of Christ's work on the cross. It also served as a reminder for me to respond to everything that happened during my day in a way that would move me toward the person I wanted to become. As I undressed in the evening, I returned the nail to my nightstand, ready to repeat the pattern the following morning. I performed this odd ritual each and every day for over a year.

So you don't think I'm *too* odd, I'm not suggesting living life as a masochistic monk. No one, at least in their right mind, should be out looking for difficulties – they seem to find us on their own. Nor should we gleefully welcome adversity when it knocks on our door. That *would* be odd. What I am suggesting is that the process of formation isn't as complicated nor as mysterious as we often make it. Our everyday routine provides endless opportunities to practice our responses in ways that shape us into the person we hope to become. This principle is true, both in our response to everyday situations in our life *and* in the everyday activities of our leadership.

To eliminate any confusion, practicing our responses isn't simply behavioral modification. As a follower of Jesus Christ, it's an intentional and consistent decision of our will, to agree with and align ourselves to our new nature, already brought about by our spiritual conversion. This process of spiritual transformation occurs by the grace of God *and* in conjunction with our responses.

Oswald Chambers explains this symbiotic relationship between God's grace and our effort with these words. "The question of forming habits on the basis of the grace of God is a very vital one. If we refuse to practice, it is not God's grace that fails when a crisis comes, but our own nature. When the crisis comes, we ask God to help us, but He cannot if we have not made our nature our ally. The practicing is ours, not God's. God regenerates us—gives us a new life—and puts us in contact with all His divine resources, but He cannot make us walk according to His will." [1]

God is so committed to this process of transformation – shaping us into the likeness of His son – that He will use *all things* toward that end. To be clear, I didn't say (nor do I believe), that God *causes everything*. I never imagined God would *allow* a tragedy such as the death of my wife, to ever occur in my life. But I quickly realized that if I would trust Him in the process, like a chisel in the hands of a gifted sculptor, He would use it, to shape me. Once I understood that God's ultimate goal for me (and my leadership), wasn't happiness, success, prosperity, or personal satisfaction (although He was not opposed to such things), but rather transformation into the likeness of His son, I began to more willingly embrace difficulty as a tool to shape me toward that end.

As Christian leaders, we know that the ultimate goal as a follower of Christ is to become more and more like the One we are following. But do we see the everyday challenges in our life and leadership as an opportunity for that shaping to occur? For many years I didn't. However, the attitude that we develop toward times of difficulty will determine the person, and the kind of leader, we become. Therefore developing a positive attitude toward these times is the fourth core idea to building a life of greater sustainability in Christian leadership.

Instead of seeing a conflict with someone under my leadership as a battle to be won, I now see it as an opportunity for my own personal growth. Instead of viewing the challenges that come with leading as just another aggravation, I now see it as an opportunity to be transformed into the image of His son. I no longer start with the attitude that the issue is about the other person or even about the problem. The issue is now about my attitude, and what God wants to do in my life through this situation. With my new attitude toward challenges and adversity, I no longer start with the thought "who is right or wrong in this situation?" or "how am I going to win this disagreement?" I now start by asking, "God, how do You want to use this situation to shape me into the image of Your son?"

What I've found is that when I consistently have un-Christlike attitudes to difficult situations in my leadership responsibilities, it's a tip off to me that something isn't right in my head or my heart. And letting that attitude go on for any length of time is similar to your car engine light coming on. It's an indication that something is not healthy and something needs to be serviced.

Unfortunately, I've seen too many Christian leaders become more twisted than transformed through their leadership journey. And honestly, I've dealt with the same challenge. But for us as Christian leaders, the question becomes: "how are we allowing the things that happen in our life and leadership shape us?" Are we becoming more hardened or more humble? Are we becoming more cynical or more gracious? Are we becoming more resentful or more thankful? Are we becoming more bitter or more compassionate?

Will we allow these times of difficulty deform us or transform us? That's the question. This process, however, doesn't happen overnight.

SLOW AND STEADY

After my late wife passed away, I was a widower for three and a half years. In December 2007, I remarried. My wife is an artist, and every time she starts a new painting, there are two critical times in the process for her. The first one is when she decides to *start*. It's during this part of the process that that little, yet loud, voice starts yelling, "You can't do this. You know the painting won't turn out right. The dimensions will be wrong. The colors won't work. Even if you do get started, you'll never finish it."

The second critical time is half way through the project. After my wife's been working really hard on a painting, and it's not coming together the way she wants, I've heard her on more than one occasion say, "I just can't do this. It looks terrible. I'm going to throw the whole thing away." Sometimes, she'll draw me into her own self-doubting dialogue and ask, "Honey, how do you think this looks? Do these colors work? Does the nose look right? Is this any good or should I just scrap it?" I find this part of the conversation a scary place to be! Usually with a nod and a few affirming words, both myself and the painting are safe – at least for another day.

The key, during these two crucial times in the process, is for my wife to keep going. She must make one brush stroke followed by another, followed by another. Try a different shade of color here; rework this part of the painting over there. Eventually, yes eventually, she finishes another beautiful painting.

I find the same with writing. When I started working on this particular chapter, I had a hard time getting started. Then, half way through the process, I wanted to toss the whole thing. The words wouldn't flow. The examples felt contrived. The chapter didn't make sense. But, after several hours and numerous revisions (although it's far from perfect) it's finally finished.

The same is true in our journey into a life of greater inner health and wholeness. It's a step by step, day by day, line by line, season by season, year by year, decade by decade process, and eventually – we look more and more like Jesus. The painting may not be perfect, but it's closer to the original than when we began.

The Church, however, isn't always that helpful in the process of personal transformation. It can be one of our biggest barriers. Here's why: Most of the Church is event-driven and encounter-oriented. And therein lies a major hurdle.

EVENT DRIVEN

Think about it. Most of our churches are built around services, meetings, conferences, seminars, concerts, classes, groups, and programs. Like a handful of marbles tossed on a table, many of these events have no purposeful relationship to a predetermined outcome. Instead, many of the activities offered in most churches are disconnected, scattered spurts of energy, with little of the end goal in mind.

Spiritual growth doesn't work that way. Personal transformation isn't found in an event, or captured in an encounter. There is no magic wand, no silver bullet, no special prayer, no secret code. The process of transformation takes the grace of God, in cooperation with our own consistent and concerted effort, with another huge dose of the grace of God, in cooperation with some more of our own consistent and concerted effort, with another dose of the grace of God, in cooperation with..... .Well you get the point. It's not one or the other. It's a both-and combination. It's God's grace working in us while we work with and in God's grace.

The Apostle Paul writes of his own symbiotic interaction between God's grace at work in his life, while he is at work in God's grace. "But by the grace of God I am what I am, and his grace to me was not without effect. No, *I worked harder than all of them* – yet not I, *but the grace of God that was with me*" (I Corinthians 15:10). As one of my mentors has said, "God *is* opposed to earning, but He's *not* opposed to effort." [2]

Like the Apostle Paul, Peter also encourages us to exert effort. In II Peter 3:18 he writes, "*grow* in the grace and knowledge of our Lord and Savior Jesus Christ." Earlier, in this same epistle, he gives us some instruction on how to do so. He writes, "...*make every effort* to add to your faith goodness; and to goodness, knowledge; and to knowledge, self-control; and to self-control, perseverance; and to perseverance, godliness; and to godliness, brotherly kindness; and to brotherly kindness, love" (2 Peter 1: 5 – 7). Now that takes effort. This idea of us doing our part while God is doing his is reinforced throughout the New Testament. [3]

ENCOUNTER ORIENTED

The hindrance in the Church to spiritual growth being a process isn't limited to our event-driven methodology. It's also reinforced by much of our encounter-oriented theology.

I was raised in the Charismatic tradition of the Church. I've been a part of this tradition for over 50 years, and pastoring within it, now, for over thirty-five years. The Charismatic expression of the Church is one which I appreciate and affirm (most of the time!). During my years in this particular expression of the Church, I've seen many people saved, healed, and delivered. I've seen the gifts of the Holy Spirit powerfully at work within a congregation. I've experienced wonderful times of anointed and animated worship. I've personally had many supernatural encounters with the Holy Spirit that have dramatically affected my life and leadership. Therefore, I sincerely believe in the present, active, authentic work of the Holy Spirit.

But, when it comes to understanding and embracing spiritual growth as a process, I believe much of the Church has done us a great disservice. Too often, we've presented and promoted spiritual growth through an encounter-oriented theology. "Come to the altar and get your miracle!" "Don't miss tonight's church service. It will change your life!" Our overemphasis on supernatural encounters has worked against the reality that spiritual growth is a process; it's a lot of hard work over a long period of time. Yes, encounters with the Holy Spirit *can be* catalytic, and at times, they *can bring* about substantive change. But generally, substantive change happens as we take small steps, in the same direction, over long periods of time. As James Houston states so well, "*The speed of gaining information is very fast, but the speed of godliness is very slow.*"[4]

As usual, Dallas Willard, explains this principle well. He writes,

> The one lesson we learn from all available sources is that there is no 'quick fix' for the human condition. The approach to wholeness is for humankind a process of great length and difficulty that engages all our own powers to their fullest extent over the long course of our experience. We are somewhat misled by the reports of experiences by many spiritual leaders, and we assign their greatness to these great moments they were given, neglecting the years of slow progress they endured before them. Thus it is necessary to say that conversion, as understood in Christian circles, is not the same thing as the required transformation of the self. The fact that a long course of experience is needed for the transformation is not set aside when we are touched by the new life from above. [5]

PRACTICE AND PERSEVERANCE

All of us like things to happen fast, but we know life doesn't usually work that way.

When we see a gymnast become an "overnight celebrity" at the Olympics, we shouldn't forget that the three minute performance of perfection that flung her to stardom was the result of thousands and thousands of hours of practice in the privacy of a gym. When Michael Phelps, at the age of 27, became the most decorated Olympian of all time, we should remember that he had logged hundreds and hundreds and hundreds of miles in the pool, stroke by stoke, day by day, and year by year, for twenty years – before he reached his status of "success." These two illustrations support what Malcom Gladwell, in his book, *Outliers*, has described as the 10,000 hours to mastery. Malcom's research shows that it takes approximately 10,000 hours of practice to master something. [6] Is it any different in our journey of spiritual transformation?

The fact is, growth and greatness are always the result of a lot of hard work over a long period of time. Our spiritual growth is no different.

All of us love a good miracle. We love the stories in the Bible of a man who couldn't walk, then suddenly can. A storm that's raging at sea, then suddenly stops. A beggar who is blind, then he can see. Yes, we like it when things happen "suddenly." Even when we think about "God sending a revival" it's usually couched in the context that it will happen "suddenly." When we pray, "Oh that you would rend the heavens and come down…," we think of revival appearing like rain. One moment it's not raining, and the next moment it is. Or, we expect revival to happen as it did with the coming of the Holy Spirit as recorded in Acts 2: "Suddenly a sound like the blowing of a violent wind came from heaven and filled the whole house…"

What we easily forget, however, is that the people of God were without the personal, indwelling work of the Holy Spirit for thousands of years. Yes, the promise of the Spirit had been given in Joel 2, but it was over 800 years before it actually happened. It "suddenly happened," but it really wasn't suddenly.

Certainly, times of "suddenlies" and "miraculous turn-arounds" are found throughout the Bible, and throughout the history of the church. And we should certainly believe for them in our own lives as well. In reality though, "suddenlies" are not the norm – neither in life nor in our spiritual walk. I've had times of breakthrough and unprecedented acceleration in my life and ministry, but usually my progress has been step by step and day by day.

IT CAME TO PASS

A friend once mentioned to me that the phrase, "and it came to pass," is in the Bible fifty times more often than the term "suddenly." I was shocked by his statement. So I did some of my own homework.

In the King James Version of the bible, the word "sudden" is only used three times and the word "suddenly" is only used 41 times. But the phrase, "and it came to pass" is used 2,761 times. Even if you add the number of times the word "immediately" is used in the Bible (55 times), to the number of times the word "sudden" or "suddenly" are used (44 times), the idea of "it came to pass" verses the idea of "suddenly" or "immediately" is still 30 to 1. This simple word study reinforces my point: spiritual growth and building a life of staying power is a process. It can't be microwaved.

Author and Pastor Eugene Peterson best describes this idea of spiritual growth as a process in the title of a book he wrote many years ago. The book's title is, A *Long Obedience in the Same Direction* and its byline is *Discipleship in an Instant Society*. Little more needs to be said.

In his book, Peterson makes these convincing and convicting observations about the process of spiritual growth. He writes:

> One aspect of (our) world that I have been able to identify as harmful to Christians is the assumption that anything worthwhile can be acquired at once. We assume that if something can be done at all, it can be done quickly and efficiently. Our attention spans have been conditioned by thirty-second commercials. Our sense of reality has been flattened by thirty-page abridgements.
>
> It is not difficult in such a world to get a person interested in the message of the gospel; it is terrifically difficult to sustain the interest. Millions of people in our culture make decisions for Christ, but there is a dreadful attrition rate. Many claim to be born again, but the evidence for mature Christian discipleship is slim. In our kind of culture anything, even news about God, can be sold if it is packaged freshly; but when it loses its novelty, it goes on the garbage heap. There is a great market for religious experience in our world; there is little enthusiasm for the patient acquisition of virtue, little inclination to sign up for a long ap-

prenticeship in what earlier generations of Christians called holiness. [7]

STEP BY STEP

Felicity Aston knows what it's like to move step by step and day by day in the same direction over a long period of time. Her journey started on November 25th, 2011. As she stood watching the plane that had just dropped her off on the edge of Antarctica quickly fade into the horizon, Aston had no idea just how difficult her journey would be.

One account of her harrowing journey is recalled with these words:

> While overcoming the initial shock [of feeling alone] may have been the greatest challenge, it was only incrementally greater than the many others Aston knew she would face. Standing became unbearable, with every muscle in her body sore from spending 12 hours a day on skis. Sitting wasn't any better; she had open sores, possibly from exposing her skin to temperatures of 40 below every time she went to the bathroom. Her ribs ached from the bloody cough caused by the dry, cold air. During the blinding storms, she became nauseated because she was so disoriented that she couldn't make out up from down. And at night, alone in her tent, she had difficulty falling asleep as she faced the dread of knowing she'd have to do it all over again tomorrow – and the next day, and the day after that. [8]

Despite exhaustion, malnutrition, frostbite, cramps, sunburn, hypothermia, crevasse fields, whiteouts, temperatures below-40 C, hurricane-speed winds, hallucinations, strange sensations, and moments of unstoppable sobbing – Felicity trekked on. Step by step, day by day, for 59 days, until after traveling 1,084 miles. On January 22, 2012 she reached her destination and her goal. At the age of 33, Felicity Aston became the first woman to ski solo across the continent of Antarctica. [9]

How did she accomplish such a remarkable feat? One step at a time, one mile at a time, one day at a time. Our growth into the likeness of Christ and into a life of greater sustainability as a Christian leader is no different.

Wherever you may be in your process of building a life of greater health and wholeness let me encourage you to take the next step and the next and the next. We can be the men and women Christ has called us to be. We can live and lead from a life of greater health and wholeness, and help those we serve do the same.

That's my goal. I trust it's yours.

ACTION AND APPLICATION

What events in your life have you experienced that have profoundly shaped you? In what ways have they shaped you?

_____

_____

Do you agree or disagree that the church is too event-driven and encounter oriented? Why or why not?

_____

_____

Do you agree or disagree that these two emphases make it more difficult to present spiritual growth as a process?

_____

_____

What are some other hindrances to the steady and slow spiritual growth in people's lives?

_____

_____

RECOMMENDED RESOURCES:

- *A Long Obedience in the Same Direction* by Eugene H. Peterson
- *Renovation of the Hearty* by Dallas Willard
- *The Life You've Always Wanted* by John Ortberg

CHAPTER TEN

TRUE CONFESSIONS OF TODAY'S CHRISTIAN CHURCH

The system is perfectly suited to create the problem we have.
JAMES BRYAN SMITH

I'm a church guy. I grew up in the church, my dad pastored for over fifty years and I've been a pastor myself for many years. I love the church, and I'm deeply committed to Her. Yet, like someone going through detox, it seems obvious that the Church is in the middle of some major convulsions. The tremors are everywhere. In fact, many are saying that we could be in the early stages of a reformation as historic as the days of Martin Luther.

The statistics supporting the church's decline are well documented. The following are only a few examples. Like the prophet Jeremiah, as you read them, may they cause you to weep.

- Over the past twenty years, every mainline Protestant church has been in significant decline.
- In the first half of the 1900's there were 27 churches for every 10,000 Americans. In 1950 there were 17 churches for every 10, 000 Americans. Today, there are less than 11 churches for every 10, 000 Americans.
- Every year approximately 4,000 churches close their doors, while approximately 1,000 new churches open their doors.
- Despite an increase in the US population of 11.4 percent over the last ten years, the combined membership of Protestant denominations decreased over the same ten years by 9.5 percent.
- Despite all the efforts of church planting and church revitalization, every year another 2.7 million church members fall into inactivity. [1]
- According to a survey by Pew Forum on Religion and Public Life, in 2012 the number of Protestants fell below the 50 percent mark for the first time in American History. [2]
- Twelve hundred Evangelicals leave the faith each day.
- Over 20 million believers no longer have anything to do with the institutional church.

There are mixed reports on how many Americans are actually still connected to the church. In studies conducted by Dave Olson, director of church planting for the Evangelical Covenant Church, his numbers from actual counts of people in Orthodox Christian churches (Catholic, mainline and evangelical) reveals that on any given weekend only 17.7 percent of the U.S. population attends church. Another study shows that since the 1970s, the share of those who never attend religious services or attend less than once a year increased by 53 percent, while those who attend several times a year or weekly decreased by 29 and 26 percent, respectively. According to the Gallup polls and other statisticians, they report that the percentage is still around 40 percent, although all would agree that of those who do attend church, they attend church much less frequently. [3] No matter how you analyze the numbers, like a skier on an alpine slope, they are all rapidly moving in a downward direction.

As someone who's grown up in the church and has been pastoring for over thirty years, I'm deeply saddened and greatly alarmed by the condition of today's Christian church. And even though I remain committed to Her, I'm not blind to the church's challenges. I certainly understand why so many people are abandoning the institutional forms of church. Believe me, there have been days when I've been tempted to turn off the lights, close the doors, and walk away. But as it's been wisely said, "Nothing was ever accomplished in a stampede!" [4] So now's not the time to walk away.

What does all of this have to do with staying power in the life of a Christian leader?

Whether we like it or not, this is the condition of the church which we serve today, and therefore, it seems impossible, and rather naïve, to discuss the condition of today's Christian leaders, without discussing the condition of today's

Christian church. I think it's reasonable to assume that the condition of one affects the condition of the other. The condition of today's church affects the health of today's Christian leaders, and the condition of today's Christian leaders affects the health of today's Christian church.

Therefore the fifth core idea to sustainability in Christian leadership is to have some honest reassessment of today's Church and respond with a clear and courageous plan of action.

Consider this: if a high percentage of workers in a factory were being frequently and repeatedly injured, wouldn't it be incomprehensible if the "powers that be" weren't willing to consider which conditions were causing the injuries? This lack of action would be unconscionable, and in most professions it would be liable.

Isn't it possible that the very models of ministry we are building, and attempting to maintain, may be the very structures and systems that are doing the damage to our health as Christian leaders? Is it possible that the church's sickness is part of the reason of our own? If so, what can we do about it?

First of all, it's important we don't incessantly whine or constantly complain about it. I've fallen into that trap, and it hasn't been helpful. As one of my professors recently said, "Leaders are like a sea captain who is called and trained to sail in the worst kind of weather. Captains don't curse the wind or wave. To this they are called. Problems are the reasons leaders exist. Without them, leaders are not needed. No whining allowed." [5]

We shouldn't whine about it, but we also shouldn't deny it. Avoiding the facts of today's declining and anemic church will only accelerate our slow death. As Robert E. Quinn in his book, *Deep Change*, warns, "Denial occurs when we are presented with painful information about ourselves, information that suggests that we need to make a deep change. Denial is one of several clear paths toward slow death. When we practice denial, we work on the wrong solution or no solutions at all. *The problem grows worse as we become discouraged, and our vitality level declines.*" [6] I must say, I've seldom seen so many pastors and Christian leaders as discouraged as I see in this season of the church.

If neither whining nor denial will help us, then what will? As Christian leaders, we must face the facts concerning the condition of today's church, with faith and a clear and courageous plan of action. We need some seasoned sea captains at the helm right now. Therefore, in this chapter and the next, we will reassess some areas in the Church and offer some actions to consider as we lead in this season of seemingly seismic shifts in today's Church.

FOUR RESPONSES

Over the past several years, as I've watched Christian leaders react to the declining condition of today's church, I've observed four basic responses.

The first response is a movement toward more programmatic, consumer-driven, activity-oriented churches. The reasoning seems to be, "let's do more and hope something works. Maybe building a bigger building with a larger stage and more bright lights, or offering more activities for the kids, will keep'em coming." I'm not sure more casual, cultural, consumer Christianity is what we need.

The second response is a movement toward hyper spirituality and revivalist rhetoric. Many of these churches talk about the way it "used to be," and long for those days to return. Don't get me wrong: I believe the church needs to be revived! But much of what we've peddled over the past few decades as revival hasn't brought the church back to life. In fact, many of these so called "revivals" have made many even more disillusioned and cynical toward today's church.

The third response is a movement toward "deconstructing the church." This movement is attempting to dismantle the "cultural baggage" that's been built up around the church over the centuries, and return to a simpler, purer form of church. Personally, I think this is a move in the right direction, as long as we keep the Bible front and center in our deconstructing efforts. Unfortunately, I'm not sure this is consistently the case.

The fourth response is a mass exodus from the church. There is something incredibly naïve and alarmingly unbiblical about the idea of abandoning the church. Being a part of the church's restoration and renewal process? Yes. Being involved in changing the church's systems and structures? Yes. But abandoning it?

If you do your homework on those who have the left the "organized church" to pursue a purer and more organic form of it – especially if you check in on some of these people a few years after they've left – you'll usually find that they aren't any closer to looking like Jesus. Neither are they having any greater impact on their world, than before they left. I know there are *some* exceptions to this observation, but trust me, I've done my homework. If you follow the stories, and check the facts, you'll find that this mass exodus hasn't furthered the "cause of Christ" nor helped reform the church of Jesus Christ.

FOUR AREAS TO CONSIDER

As I've wrestled with the declining condition of today's Church, my struggle has brought me to some new conclusions *and* some old convictions. Following are four areas to consider as we lead in these changing times.

A Needed Reformation

The first thing I'm convinced of is that this time of transition in the church is a needed one. Even though it's a treacherous and tumultuous time for many of us, I believe God is at work.

Patterns of decline and renewal aren't anything new in the history of the church. God's people – both in the biblical narrative and throughout the history of the church – have repeatedly gone through times of wandering and times of returning, times of slumber and times of great awakening. Whether from the days of Josiah to the days of Jeremiah, or from the days of Martin Luther to the days of Martin Luther King – God's people have repeated the pattern of decline and rebirth, near extinction and miraculous resurrection.

I'm convinced that the church today, while still in the hands of a gracious God and under the watchful eye of a faithful Father, is in the beginning phase of another one of God's great restoration projects. However, like any construction project, sometimes you have to tear down before you can build up. In this process, the building always gets uglier before it becomes beautiful.

Phyllis Tickle, in her book, *The Great Emergence: How Christianity Is Changing and Why*, proposes that about every 500 years the church goes through a "great" transformation. She supports her premise by counting back 500 years from the present to the Great Reformation, and then 500 hundred years prior to the Great Reformation to the Great Schism, and then five hundred years from the Great Schism to the monastic movement, and then five hundred years from the monastic movement to the first century and to the time of the apostles.

Tickle proposes that, "About every five hundred years the empowered structures of institutional Christianity, whatever they may be at the time, become an intolerable carapace [exterior] that must be shattered in order that renewal and new growth may occur." She further makes the observation that when these cycles of upheaval in the history of the church occur, there are always at least three consistent results:

- A more vital form of Christianity emerges
- The organized expression of Christianity becomes more pure
- The Church ends up with two new expressions rather than one

She contends that the church is in the throes of another great transformation. [7] I, along with many others, fully agree. I believe God is at work. He is reshaping His Church.

A Renewed Ecclesiology

The second thing I'm convinced of is that during this time of transition, we need to return to a clear, biblical theology *of* the church.

As I've stated earlier, I totally agree that many of the voices challenging today's Church are needed. I honestly understand why people are so disappointed with the church, and abandoning the institutional forms of it. There are certainly many issues in the church that need to be addressed. What I am cautious and concerned about, however, is that many of the ideas being offered as remedies aren't being initiated by a clear biblical theology of the church. Instead, many of the proposed remedies seem to be driven more by personal preferences, practical pragmatism, compliances to cultural pressures, or catering to consumer demands. In the long-run, changes made on these fickle grounds won't be that helpful.

Many of the remedies seem to focus more on style or structure, and less on substance. More candles and less choirs, more "organic" and less organizational, more spontaneity and less liturgy (or in some cases more liturgy and less spontaneity), more dialogue and less monologue, more story and less didactic, more experiential and less doctrinal, more comfort and less cost, more entertainment and less commitment, and the list goes on.

I fully believe that the current conversations about re-shaping the church are needed, but my concern is that concentrating on these external modifications may be missing the mark. Are we focusing on a face-lift when a heart transplant is needed?

In a book Chuck Colson wrote several years ago titled *The Body*, he describes the church's identity crisis with these insightful words.

> No perception is more firmly rooted in our culture than that the church is a building – a view held by both church and unchurched. It's no surprise that nonbelievers don't really know much about the church's identity or mission. *But when Christians themselves are undergoing a widespread identity crisis, then we are in big trouble. For this confusion strips the church of its authority...* The hard truth is that we have substituted an institutional religion for the life-changing dynamic of a living faith. *Therefore, there isn't a more urgent or critical task than the recovery and restoration of the biblical view of the church.*[8]

I would appeal that a return to the Bible and what *God instructs us to do* as followers of Jesus Christ and participating members in the body of Christ, *must be* the motivation *for*, and the blueprint *from* which the church is reshaped.

Let me be clear here. I do believe that returning to the biblical understanding of the church will result in many of the programs, practices and structures of the church being reshaped. Let's just make sure we start with the root issues and work our way out from there. Simply reshuffling the chairs on the deck of a sinking ship won't remedy the problem. We need to right the ship!

A Reconnection To Christ As Our Head

The third thing I'm convinced of is that we must return Christ to the head of the church.

Although God gives responsibilities of leadership to men and women within His Church, we must consistently and passionately look to Jesus as our sole source and single leader. Like a faulty GPS, relying on any other source will only get us lost and lead us straight into more dead religion. Jesus is the life and leader of the church; it's to him that we must remain intimately connected.

Ed Hayes, in his book *The Church*, writes these words of warning regarding the headship of Christ in His Church. "If institutionalism is to be avoided, focus on the headship of Jesus Christ in His Church is pivotal. An adequate grasp of this principle will serve to correct and safeguard against *either* pastoral or lay abuse of power. Furthermore it may keep us from giving undue attention to the structure of the church – its buildings and governance – over proper attention to prayer, worship and guidance by the Holy Spirit." [9] Another writer pointedly puts it this way, "We must never forget that the hope of the church rests not on its own strategies and wisdom but on the *living God alone...*" [10] Yes!

As Christian leaders, we agree *doctrinally* that Christ is the head of the church. Many times, though, we don't lead according to what we say we believe. Instead of seeking His direction by listening to what He is saying and watching what He is doing, we, more often than not, run the church by leadership and management practices adopted from current corporate models. I'm not suggesting many of these practices aren't' needed or important. They are. Having a clear vision with a corresponding strategy, having the right people in the right place doing the right things, accompanied by efficient structures that help us manage our vision and measure our effectiveness – are all important. My appeal is that these practices should be implemented *in response* to *what* God is saying to us and *where* God is leading us, and not as a replacement *of* His leading of us.

One of the best definitions on spiritual leadership I've ever read was proposed by Dr. Henry and Richard Blackaby. In their book, *Spiritual Leadership,* they define spiritual leadership *as moving people on to God's agenda.*[11] This is a great definition. However, the definition implies that a spiritual leader must first know what God's agenda *is*, and *then* use strategic and spirit enabled leadership to determine how to best lead people there.

I was at a conference a few years ago where one of the great statesmen of the church was asked during an interview, "What's your greatest concern for the church in America?" His response, "We have come to believe that if we build the right structures, offer the right programs, and do the right marketing, we can build a successful church without needing much help from God." (Ouch!)

My concern is that (more than we'd like to admit it) we are building people into either a corporate church vision, or a charismatic leader, or a belief system, or a denominational structure, or a religious cause – instead of building people into Jesus Christ. It's imperative that we do what Jesus reminded us to do: *remain connected to the vine* (John 15: 1-17). And do what Paul exhorted us to do: *be built up into Christ* (Ephesians 4:15; Colossians 1:28-29; 2: 6-7; 2:19). Anything less than this is a disservice to those we are called to serve.

A Renewed Commitment To The Church

The last thing I'm convinced of is that even during this time of turbulence and transition, God is still *very* committed to His Church.

I've been fortunate to travel to churches in Asia, Africa, Europe, South America, Canada and all across the U.S. I've been with God's people congregated in cathedrals, huddled in huts, sitting in stadiums, hiding in tents, gathered in auditoriums, and meeting in open fields. I've been in the State Church, underground church, Free Church, high church, subdued church, wild church, white church, black church, Hispanic church, Asian church, and Indian church. I've been in churches where the men sat on one side and the women on the other. I've been in churches where you had to wear a coat and tie to preach, and in churches where people thought you were weird if you did wear a coat and a tie when you preached. I've heard some great preachers in places all around the world, and I've heard some that weren't so great. I've been in churches where God seemed near, and in some where He didn't seem to be anywhere.

One thing my travels have convinced me of is that God isn't all that concerned with the various forms of the church. He isn't enamored with our church programs, impressed by our organizational structures, or committed to our institutional systems. But God is still *very, very* committed to His Church.

It was December 8, 2007 and I stood waiting in the front of the auditorium. My heart was beating as though I'd just finished a hundred-yard dash. The music soars, the double doors in the back of the sanctuary swing open, necks crane and like a well-trained church choir, in unison the congregation rises. I catch a glimpse of white and start to smile, and then start to cry. There she is my new bride.

My experience in that moving and magical moment hints at the same passion Christ has for His Church. He loves us so much that he calls us His Bride. But for many of us, the idea and imagery of the church being a "bride" is a hard one to grasp – primarily for two reasons.

The first reason is because of her ugliness. Unfortunately over the years, we've seen more of her faults and failures, sins and shortcomings, warts and wanderings than we've seen of her love and compassion, justice and mercy, humility and unity. We've often seen more of her ugliness than her beauty. As one author writes, "More people have been brought into the church by the kindness of real Christian love than by all the theological arguments in the world; and more people have been driven from the church by the hardness and ugliness of so-called Christianity than by all the doubts in the world." [12]

The second reason it's often difficult to see the church as a bride is because of her adultery. Instead of seeing the church as being faithful to her vows of purity and fidelity, we've too often watched as she has wandered off after other lovers. Many years ago a close friend – one of the godliest women I've ever known – had a dream in which she was in bed with a well-known Hollywood leading man. In her dream, although still fully dressed, she was gently fondling his face as they lay lustfully looking into each other's eyes. When she awoke, she immediately knew the meaning of the dream. *The church had once again left her first love and was being seduced by another lover.* It's grievous, but true. Like a nymphomaniac, our harlotry that started in the garden, still runs in our veins. God help us, we are so easily seduced.

When we look at the Bride from a human perspective, all her deformities easily stand out. We seem to see nothing but the warts on her nose, corns on her toes, and bulges in places they don't belong. But, when we consider the church from a heavenly perspective – from God's vantage point – we are reminded that the church, although far from perfect, is still in process, and will continue to be until her perfect Bridegroom returns. No, this doesn't excuse our immaturity or ugliness, and it doesn't justify our idolatry or adultery. It does, however, provide us with a picture of what the church could be, and it gives us hope for what the church one day will be.

I'm told if you visit the Galleria dell' Accàdemia in Florence Italy, you will find Michelangelo's masterpiece, *the statue of David,* standing next to four unfinished and ugly marble statues of slaves. One writer uses this picture as an example of what the church currently looks like compared to what the church will one day become. He writes:

> The church, God's greatest community of hope, is something like the four unfinished marble status of slaves the sculptor Michelangelo began in sixteenth-century Florence. The characters cry to be

released from their prison of roughhewn stone, but the vision of what they were to become died with the artist. Those crude and ghostly shapes will never know the perfection of Michelangelo's greatest work, *David.* In the Galleria dell' Accadèmia... the perfect and the imperfect stand in stark contrast.

The church, while imperfect and incomplete, is still being shaped by its living Master, Jesus Christ. This same Lord has promised that one day He will present His bride, *'as a radiant church, without stain or wrinkle or any other blemish, but holy and blameless'* (Ephesians 5:27). En route to the final consummation of the age, the church lives as a prisoner of hope, expecting the return of Jesus Christ. [13]

I get very concerned with people who are constantly throwing stones at Christ's Bride. Have we done some really reprehensible and insanely stupid things throughout the history of the church? Yes. Does the church need restoration and renewal? Yes. Is she going through a season of reformation, bordering on a revolution? Yes.

I'm not suggesting we turn a blind eye to areas in the church that need correcting; nor sit by while corruption and compromise continues. I'm certainly not suggesting we give up on the church, or give in to some faithless and fatalistic ecclesiology. I do recommend, however, that we don't marginalize what God has made central, make small what God has made large, or despise what God deeply adores. Jesus is still deeply in love with His Bride. He loves us so much so that He gave his very life for us and He continues to long for us as He daily intercedes for us. God loves His Church. He is ruthlessly committed to His Bride. And you and I must be as well!

As we reassess today's Christian church and respond with a clear and courageous plan, our staying power as Christian leaders will be strengthened. Yet, there is one more thing we must consider and we turn to that now.

ACTION AND APPLICATION

Do you believe the statistics in this chapter properly represents the condition of today's Christian church? Yes. No. What condition do you believe the church is in? Why?

_____

_____

Of the four responses I presented to the condition of today's Christian church, which one do you see occurring the most:

❑ More consumer driven models   ❑ Revivalist models

❑ Deconstruction Models   ❑ Abandonment of the Church

Of the four areas I presented for us to reconsider during this season of the church, which one(s) resonates most? And why?

_____

_____

Where is your current "love" and commitment level toward the Church? Is it high, low, passionate, apathetic, hopeful, disappointed, etc.? Why?

_____

_____

RECOMMENDED RESOURCES:

- *Giving Church Another Chance* by Todd Hunter
- *Renovation of the Church* by Ken Carlson and Mike Lueken
- *The Church* by Ed Hayes

CHAPTER ELEVEN

FINDING OUR FOCUS

Could the reason that the failure in the Christian world is occurring, is not in spite of what we are doing, but precisely because of it?

DALLAS WILLARD

I was recently playing golf with three bankers. These were new acquaintances, so we were getting to know one another by making "small talk." I was preparing to tee off on the seventh hole when one of them casually asked, "Pastor Ken, tell me, what would you say is your greatest challenge in pastoring today?"

I thought for a moment. I could say, "Dealing with divisive and mean spirited people." But that's really not that much of a challenge. Or, I could say, "Dealing with people's ongoing sin and moral compromise, and the mess it gets them in." There would be some truth to that, but still not my greatest challenge. I thought a bit longer. I could say, "Dealing with people's apathy toward God and their lack of intentionality toward their spiritual growth." Now, that would be close to my biggest challenge.

Just before I stepped to the tee box and hit a 250 yard drive deep into the woods, I replied, "My biggest challenge is distractions."

People are so distracted by life that they are going in multiple directions and that spills over into the lack of focus in the life of the church. In fact, when I think about my own leadership within the church, I'm stunned by how much energy I've exerted over matters that are really not that important. There are so many things to do, so many needs to fulfill, so many things to get done, so many ideas to pursue, so many meetings to attend, so many activities to administrate, so many programs to promote, so many... Well, so many of everything. When you add that to the fact that people are incredibly busy and have endless things coming at them – obligations, pressures, options, etc. Without a doubt, distraction is my greatest challenge leading in today's church. I think many of my colleagues would agree.

Since Satan is the ultimate illusionist, could it be that, like any good magician, his sleight of hand trick is to distract us? Is it possible that he has gotten us to "major on the minors" and neglect the most important areas of ministry? Could it be that we are focusing on less important matters, while the things that matter most to the life and mission of the church, go unaddressed? What would happen if we flipped this? What would happen if, instead of giving our energy to the many things we are distracted by, we gave our efforts to what's most essential?

Leith Anderson, a longtime pastor and fellow thinker on the condition of today's church, offers this insight for us to consider. He writes,

> While the New Testament speaks often about churches, it is surprisingly silent about many matters that we associate with church structure and life. There is no mention of architecture, pulpits, lengths of sermons, rules for having Sunday school. Little is said about style of music, order of worship, or times of church gatherings. There were no Bibles, denominations, camps, pastor's conferences, or board meeting minutes. Those who strive to be New Testament churches must seek to live its principles and absolutes, *not reproduce the details!* [1]

If facing the facts of today's Christian church will increase our staying power, then finding our focus will help us do the same. There is a clear correlation here. Healthy leaders build healthy organizations and healthy organizations produce healthy leaders.

Over the last few years, the church I pastor has wrestled with this question concerning focus. We've asked ourselves, in the midst of all the options, presented both as opportunities and expectations, *what do we understand – both biblically and functionally – as the essentials of the church?* Since, there are many legitimate things a church *can* do, and certainly there are a number of beneficial things a church *could* do, what *must* a church *do* to be biblically faithful and effective?

As we've worked through this question we've reduced the

options to three: a call to discipleship, a call to community, and a call to mission.

A CALL TO DISCIPLESHIP

Several years ago the church I was pastoring made a decision to no longer use the term "Christian" as the primary way to describe our spiritual journey. We made this decision for two reasons, but both boil down to people's interpretation of the term "Christian."

First, there is a lot of cultural baggage, both inside and outside the church, surrounding the term. For many the term simply means that Christianity – as opposed to Hinduism, Buddhism, Judaism, Atheism, or a host of other options – is the person's religion of choice. Those who fall into this category approach "being a Christian" as synonymous with "being an American," loving baseball, eating apple pie, and occasionally attending church on Christmas, Easter, or during a personal or national crisis.

Second, for many people, the idea of "being a Christian" means that in some fundamental way a person has accepted the basic doctrine that Jesus died on a cross so that we could be forgiven of our sins and end up in heaven one day. This understanding is a start in the right direction, but unfortunately it is only that – a start. Those who live this brand of Christianity seldom travel to the depth of what it really means to follow Christ – a journey that ultimately transforms the very essence of who we are, what we believe, and how we live.

Dallas Willard called it "vampire Christianity," and explained it this way. "Vampire Christianity is in essence when a person says to Jesus, 'I'd like a little of your blood, please. But I don't care to be your student (disciple) or have your character. In fact, won't you just excuse me while I get on with my life, and I'll see you in heaven.' " [2] Wow!

One thing that's critical concerning helping people become disciples of Jesus, and not simply making converts to cultural Christianity, is to understand the difference between the two. A cultural Christian is someone who has accepted the work of salvation secured through Christ, and has given mental assent to the Christian faith (belief system) as their religion of choice. A disciple, however, is someone who has trusted Jesus with their whole life, continues to be in relationship with Him, as they learn to be like Him, while they are on mission with Him. A cultural Christian and a disciple of Jesus Christ are worlds apart.

At some point, a heresy entered into the American church that proposes that a person can be a "Christian" without being a disciple. This faulty theology has done, and is doing, serious damage to the church, and our witness to the world.

Over 50 years ago, A.W. Tozer, one of the great Christian thinkers and prophetic voices of the 20th century, warned us of this heresy. He writes,

> … a notable heresy has come into being throughout evangelical Christian circles – the widely accepted concept that we humans can choose to accept Christ only because we need him as Savior and that we have the right to postpone our obedience to him as Lord as long as we want! Tozer goes on to state, that

salvation apart from obedience is unknown in the sacred scriptures. [3]

Dietrich Bonhoeffer expressed the same concern and coined the phrase "cheap grace" as a way to explain his concern. Bonhoeffer writes,

> Cheap grace is the preaching of forgiveness without requiring repentance, baptism without church discipline, Communion without confession.... Cheap grace is grace without discipleship, grace without the cross, grace without Jesus Christ, living and incarnate. [4]

To our own detriment, we have overemphasized being a convert, and downplayed being a disciple, resulting in a consumer Christianity that's produced anemic faith in the lives of many professing "Christians," and left little lasting impact on our world. Like our national debt, the cost of amassing converts without making disciples has caught up to us. Unless we make some radical readjustments, "Christianity" and the church's future doesn't look very bright.

It seems to me (and many others), that if we don't get the task of making disciples right, then everything else we feverishly attempt to do in the church will be off course, and inevitably fall short. As theologian and forward thinker Alan Hirsch has said, "If we fail at this point (discipleship) then we fail in all others." [5]

I define the call to discipleship as the "first button principle." If the first button on your shirt isn't in its right place, then nothing else lines up right. I'm not suggesting that many of the things we're attempting to do in our churches are being done with wrong motives. But, I am suggesting that, without discipleship at the core, everything else we attempt to do, won't produce the lasting fruit that we are all laboring and longing for.

Most Christian leaders I talk with candidly confess that with all the efforts, energies, activities, programs, conferences, seminars, services, money, and buildings and with all the preaching, teaching, leading, praying, and pleading – we are not making disciples.

Through my own experience as a pastor and Christian leader, I have come to the conclusion that of all the other things a church *can* do, making disciples is the number one thing a church *must* do.

A CALL TO COMMUNITY

The church's mission isn't only to call people to discipleship, but it's also to call people into authentic Christian community.

We see this life-together-in-community take shape in Acts chapter 2. As Peter stood and declared the gospel, those who heard the message responded and repented. They turned from one way of life and entered into a new way of life. They freely joined this first century band of disciples.

It's important to note that the attraction *to* the gospel Peter preached that day wasn't *only* because of the kind of gospel he *preached,* it was *also* because of the kind of gospel the first century Christian community *lived!* Because of the radical work of the gospel working in their lives, they were living a quality of life that provoked their watching world to wonder. Their neighbors, family, and friends *saw* the gospel in action. They saw the gospel being lived out. The kind of life that the first century Christian community lived was both an *attraction to* the gospel, and an *authentication of* the gospel. As a result, more and more people joined them on their journey.

One writer explains the quality of life that was being lived out among the first century Christian community, with these words:

> When the early church *visibly* demonstrated that all the racial and social barriers had been broken by the cross of Christ, and that through the power of the spirit, people from every background were now one in Christ, there could have been no greater evidence for the truth of the gospel in the ancient world. [6]

A second century historian who was trying to explain who these followers of Jesus Christ were to the Roman Emperor Hadrian; describes them to him this way:

> They love one another. They never fail to help widows; they save orphans from those who would hurt them. If they have something they give freely to the man who has nothing; if they see a stranger, they take him home, and are happy, as though they were a real brother. They don't consider themselves brothers in the usual sense, but brothers instead through the Spirit, in God. [7]

Don't miss this point: The clarity of the gospel we preach determines the quality of the community we create. Shallow Christians equal shallow community. Authentic followers equals authentic community. Carnal Christians equals carnal community.

Don't misunderstand me here. For a short season, a church can experience great "fellowship." We can have nice meals together, or build friendships in our small groups, or have fun at different church activities (and there's nothing wrong with that). But, if we aren't growing as disciples of Jesus Christ over time, then the authentic and loving relationships we hope to experience in "Christian community" often deteriorate into patterns of pettiness, or messy times of meanness. When this happens, our shared-life-together almost always implodes or explodes. I've seen this happen over and over.

Why is that? Why is it that so many churches do not experience the depth of life-together-in-relationships that they desperately desire? Could it be that the depth of our fellowship is determined by the depth of our discipleship? Could it be that the quality of our commitments to one another directly correlates to our commitment to Christ?

It's important to understand that this call to community isn't a minor issue. In fact, Francis Schaeffer, one of the great evangelical thinkers of the last century, once said that the world witnessing authentic spiritual community could be the last apologetic (credible evidence) of the Christian faith. [8] What he meant is that in a post-Christian and post-modern world, people not only need to *hear* the gospel preached, but they must *see* the gospel lived. And there is no greater evidence of the gospel than when it's *seen* fully functioning in an authentic spiritual community!

Just as Jesus said that his first century disciples would be known by their "love for one another," he desires (and expects) the same to be said of those who follow him today. This is why "consumer Christianity" is an oxymoron. It's antithetical to the gospel. Jesus came to save us *from* ourselves so that we can serve others, and by serving others, be a witness to our world. A "me-centered" gospel is *not* the gospel. A gospel that focuses on my consumption primarily for my happiness – isn't the gospel. It may be a self-help program with a little Christianity sprinkled in, but it's not the gospel.

A call to community is no small thing. Jesus expects it of us. The gospel demands it of us, and our culture needs to see it in us.

A CALL TO MISSION

The church's third non-negotiable is a call to mission.

Before we jump ahead too quickly on this point, it's important that we first understand specifically what our call to mission is. Historically, it's been too easy to make the church's mission too simplistic – "Let's go win the world." Or, we've made our call to mission only two dimensional: evangelism and missions. But our call to mission is much broader than that. Yes, our mission is about evangelism, it's about helping the poor; it's about "being salt and light." Yes, we are to defend the oppressed and stand up against issues of injustice. Our mission is about all of these things, but it's not limited to any one of these things.

Our mission is to be at work with God – wherever and in whatever way He is at work in our world. Our mission is really a continuation of the Incarnation. Just as the Father has sent Jesus into the world, Jesus sends us into the world (John 17:18; Acts 1:8; I Peter 2:9 – 12: Titus 2:14). As authentic followers of Jesus Christ, it is our responsibility to be Christ's presence in our world, which encompasses all of God's work, in all of God's world.

Irrespective of a person's religious persuasion, economic status, cultural background, or lifestyle choices, those of us who have committed our lives to Jesus will use what we have to help others. Whether it's the people living under our own roof, or people living across the street; whether it's people living in a homeless shelter, or an uptown penthouse; whether its people living in a refugee camp, or those who occupy the White House, being on mission with God will be as natural as the flowing in and flowing out of the ocean's tide.

Being on mission with God may be about serving the poor, giving to missions, building an orphanage, standing up for issues of injustice, providing shelter for the homeless, sharing our faith with a friend, showing hospitality to a stranger, helping plant a new church, teaching in a Sunday school class, serving in the nursery, building a home for someone in need, or sponsoring a child in a village around the world. Whatever level of activity it is, and wherever it is, as the church of Jesus Christ, we will be on mission with God!

SEQUENTIAL AND CONSEQUENTIAL

In the 1980's, I was part of a church that saw hundreds of people coming to Christ. We water baptized multitudes of people in bath tubs all across the city of Cleveland, Ohio, and the surrounding Northeast Ohio area. It was a remarkable time in ministry. Looking back, I now realize that one of the reasons we saw so many people coming to Christ was because of the clarity of the gospel that was being preached, the response to the gospel with radical repentance that was taking place, and the depth of "Christian community" that we were experiencing. Oh, may that day return!

It's important to understand that each one of these essential calls of the church have a sequential and consequential effect on the other. Each one feeds the other. A call to discipleship affects authentic community, and authentic community affects our call to mission. When these three calls remain central in the life of the church, I believe we will once again become the people who the Thessalonians described as; "those who have turned the world upside down have come here also" (Acts 17:6).

Oh may it be so!

ACTION AND APPLICATION

Do you agree that dealing with distraction is one of the greatest challenges in leading in today's church? Yes. No. Why or why not.

_____

_____

What is your greatest challenge in leading in today's church? Why?

_____

_____

Which one of the 3 essentials calls that I presented is weakest or strongest in the church or ministry you lead?

❑ A Call To Discipleship   ❑ A Call To Community
❑ A Call To Mission

What can you and your team do to strengthen these areas in the ministries that you lead?

_____

_____

RECOMMENDED RESOURCES:
• _The Great Omission_ by Dallas Willard
• _Renovation of the Church_ by Ken Carlson and Mike Lueken
• _Discipleshift_ by Jim Putman and Bobby Harrington

CHAPTER TWELVE

IF I SHOULD DIE

You never know how much you really believe anything until its truth becomes a matter of life and death to you.

C.S. LEWIS

It was a bleak, wintry day, and I was already a bit blue. The snow machine off Lake Erie had kicked in, and I was driving under gray skies into the west side of downtown Cleveland, Ohio. This once bright and promising *Leave It To Beaver* neighborhood of the 1950's, was now stained from wear, and the snow and cold only added to the dreary scene.

I drove through the slush, found my way to the well-used funeral home, stepped inside the dark foyer, with the organ dirge already droning; that's when my day got even more bleak.

I had made a commitment to someone I barely knew, to officiate the funeral of someone that the person I barely knew, barely knew. It turned out that the funeral was for an old man who had lived well into his 90's. Here's where the day gets even more depressing.

Only nine people showed up for the funeral and seven of them were forced to.

Evidently, the old man had not only been really old, but he had also been really mean. And no one – absolutely no one – had anything good to say about the man lying in the box up front (can you say "awkward?"). I certainly wasn't going to make something up, so I read a few scriptures (that's always safe), did a short prayer (also safe), then rolled him to the hearse, drove to the cemetery, lowered him into the ground, and threw some dirt on him.

That was it. A life lived. A legacy left.

As I drove home that day, I decided then and there that I would live my life in a way that counts. And by the grace of God (and some really hard work) – I believe I have.

But I'm facing a dilemma right now.

I'm at an age and stage in my life and ministry where my biggest temptation is to avoid making waves. Just continue doing what I'm doing, pick up my paycheck, and eventually ride into the sunset on my Harley with my pony tail blowing in the wind. (*I don't have a Harley or any hair, so I'm not sure how that's going to happen. But you get the idea.*) I'm at a season in life where it's really tempting to accept things as they are and just coast on through.

But I can't do that.

I want to live the rest of my life with purpose and passion for Christ and the Church. I want to continue to grow more and more into the image of His son, and I want to lead in such a way that I'm helping other Christian leaders do the same.

I'm not planning on dying any time soon, but when I do, I

already know what words I want inscribed on my tombstone. They come from a paraphrase of Hebrews 11:13. When I die and they put me in the grave, I want the words on my tombstone to read:

Kenneth Lee Roberts

Born: 11/27/56　　　*A Man Who Died*　　　**Died:**

Leaning Forward

For the remaining years of my life, this is how I want to live – this is how I want to die.

How about you? As a Christian leader in the church of Jesus Christ, what will you live for? What will you die for?

In the early 1900's, two missionaries were returning home to America from a foreign land where they had served for many years. During their crossing of the Atlantic, they dreamed of what it would be like once they reached home. They had long anticipated this day.

As the ship entered New York harbor and approached the dock, they heard a brass band playing, and saw a crowd of people waving banners and cheering. Their hearts rose, but quickly fell when they realized the fanfare wasn't for them, but for a U.S. dignitary on the ship, also returning home.

The two missionaries disembarked and made their way through the cheering crowd. One looked at the other and said, "No one was here to welcome us home. There were no bands playing or people waving banners to greet us at our arrival." His colleague turned and looked at him and said, "But my friend, we're not home yet!"

My friend, colleague and co-laborer, we are not home yet. Let's live in such a way that our lives will continue to be shaped into the image of His Son and let's lead in such a way that the Church will return to what She was originally called to be and called to do.

I pray for God's ongoing sustainability and staying power in your life and leadership.

Leaning Forward,

Ken L Roberts

NOTES

Chapter One – True Confessions Of Today's Christian Leaders

1. Wayne Cordeiro, *Leading On Empty* (Bloomington, MN: Bethany House Publishers, 2009), 21-23.

2. Doug Bannister, *Sacred Quest* (Grand Rapids, MI: Zondervan, 2001), 33-34.

3. H.B. London Jr. and Neil B. Wiseman, *Pastors at Greater Risk* (Ventura, CA: Regal Books, 2003), 20, 86, 118, 148, 172, 264.

4. "It Does Not Have To Be This Way," Gateway Collegium, 11th March. 2014. (quoting stats from The Fuller Institute: George Barna and Pastoral Care Inc. 2008 Report).

5. Ruth Haley Barton, *Sacred Rhythms,* (Downers Grove, IL: InterVarsity Press, 2006), 13.

Chapter Two – Looking Below The Waterline

1. Barbara Lloyd, "Solo Sailor Is Presumed To Be Dead," New York Times, 26 Nov. 1992.

2. Peter Scazzero, *Emotionally Healthy Spirituality* (Nashville, TN: Thomas Nelson, 2006), 88-89.

3. Dallas Willard, *The Great Omission* (New York, NY: HarperCollins Publishers, 2006), 124.

4. Dr. Gordon L. Anderson, "Lecture on The Spirit Of The Disciplines," 29 March. 2014

5. John Ortberg, *The Life You've Always Wanted* (Grand Rapids, MI: Zondervan, 1997), 86.

6. Richard Foster and Gary Beebe, *Longing For God* (Downers Grove, IL: InterVarsity Press, 2009), 73-74.

Chapter Three – Travelers Beware

1. John Stott, *The Radical Disciple* (Downers Grove, IL: InterVarsity Press, 2010), 24-25.
2. Jack Minor, "Pedophiles Want Same Rights As Homosexuals," <u>North Colorado Gazette,</u> 3 July. 2011.
3. David G. Benner, *The Gift Of Being Yourself* (Downers Grove, IL: InterVarsity Press, 2004), 13.
4. Ibid., 110.
5. Ibid., 110.
6. Ibid., 110
7. John Owen, *Overcoming Sin And Temptation* (Wheaton, IL: Crossway Books, 2006), 238.

Chapter Four – Pretending As A Profession

1. John Eldredge, *Wild At Heart* (Nashville, TN: Thomas Nelson, 2001), 54.
2. David G. Benner, *The Gift Of Being Yourself* (Downers Grove, IL: InterVarsity Press, 2004), 53-54.
3. Ruth Haley Barton, "The Wilderness Within," <u>Transforming Center email newsletter</u>, 30th March. 2011.
4. Brennan Manning, *The Ragamuffin Gospel* (Colorado Springs, CO: Multnomah Books, 1990), 134.
5. John 8:32 (author's paraphrase).
6. Sarah Bradford, *Scenes In the Life of Harriet Tubman* (Auburn, NY: W.J. Moses Printer, 1869).

7. Peter Scazzero, *Emotionally Healthy Spirituality* (Nashville, TN: Thomas Nelson, 2006), 79.

8. Kenneth Boa, *A Taste of the Classics*, vol. 1. (Colorado Springs, CO: Biblica Publishing, 2010), 25.

9. David G. Benner, *The Gift Of Being Yourself* (Downers Grove, IL: InterVarsity Press, 2004), 20-21.

Chapter Five – Why Are We So Sick?

1. Dr. F.A. Carranza, "The Discovery of Anesthesia," and R.J. Wolfe, "Tarnished Idol: A Chronicle of the Ether Controversy (San Anselmo, CA: Norman Publishing, 2001).

2. Dallas Willard, *Renovation of the Heart* (Colorado Springs, CO: NavPress, 2002), 238.

3. "It Does Not Have To Be This Way," <u>Gateway Collegium</u>, 11th March. 2014. (quoting stats from The Fuller Institute: George Barna and Pastoral Care Inc. 2008 Report).

4. Daniel Sherman, "Pastor Burnout by the Numbers," <u>PastorBurnout.com</u>

5. Dallas Willard, *Living In Christ's Presence* (Downers Grove, IL: InterVarsity Press, 2014), 15.

Chapter Six – It's Elementary My Dear Watson

1. John Stott, *The Radical Disciple* (Downers Grove, IL: InterVarsity Press, 2010), 83.

2. David G. Benner, *The Gift Of Being Yourself* (Downers Grove, IL: InterVarsity Press, 2004), 49.

3. Mark Batterson, *Soul Print* (Colorado Springs, CO: Multnomah Books, 2011), 104-105.

4. Ibid., 2.

5. M. Basil Pennington, *True Self/False Self* (New York, NY: Crossroad, 2000), 37.

6. Russell D. Moore, *Tempted and Tried* (Wheaton, IL: Crossway Books, 2011), 30-31.

7. John 5:36; Matt. 3:17; John 14:11; John 17:24

Chapter Seven – Calling All Sea Captains

1. W.A. Criswell, *Criswell's Guidebook for Pastors* (Nashville, TN: Broadman, 1980), 345.

2. Howard F. Sugden and Warren W. Wiersbe, *When Pastors Wonder How* (Chicago, IL: Moody, 1973), 9.

3. Charles Bridges, *The Christian Ministry* (Carlisle, PA: The Banner Of Truth Trust, 1991), 90.

4. I Corinthians 9:3; I Corinthians 16:9; II Corinthians 7:5, II Corinthians 11: 28-29; II Timothy 4:14,16

5. Eugene Peterson, *The Contemplative Pastor* (Grand Rapids, MI: Eerdmans, 1989), 16.

6. Ibid., 55-57.

7. John MacArthur, *Rediscovering Pastoral Ministry* (Dallas, TX: Word, 1995), 4-5.

Chapter Eight – A Few More Silent Preachers

1. Foster, Richard, ed. *The Renovaré Spiritual Formation Bible*. New York, NY: HarperCollins, 2005, 2312.

2. Ibid., 2313

3. Henri Nouwen, *Making All Things New* (San Francisco, CA: Harper and Row, 1981), 69.

4. Dallas Willard, *The Spirit Of The Disciplines* (San Francisco, CA: HarperCollins, 1988), 101.

5. Ruth Haley Barton, *Invitation To Solitude and Silence* (Downers Grove, IL: InterVarsity Press, 2004), 17.

6. Ruth Haley Barton, *Sacred Rhythms* (Downers Grove, IL: InterVarsity Press, 2006), 29.

7. Ibid., 33.

8. Article, <u>Pollution</u>, Blogspot.com, January, 2011.

9. Mark Buchanan, *The Rest Of God* (Nashville, TN: Thomas Nelson, 2006), 196.

10. Terry Hershey, *The Power Of Pause* (Chicago, IL: Loyola Press, 2009), xix.

11. Henri Nouwen, *Seeds Of Hope* (New York, NY: Doubleday, 1997), 54.

12. Thomas Merton, *New Seeds Of Contemplation* (Boston, MA: Shambhala Publications, 1961), 56.

13. Dietrich Bonhoeffer, *Life Together* (San Francisco, CA: Harper and Row, 1954), 78.

14. J. Robert Clinton, *The Making Of A Leader* (Colorado Springs, CO: NavPress, 1988), 158-162.

15. A.W. Tozer, *The Pursuit of God* (Harrisburg, PA: Christian Publications, Inc., 1948), 43.77.

16. Mark Buchanan, *The Rest Of God* (Nashville, TN: Thomas Nelson, 2006), 177-178.

17. J. Robert Clinton, *The Making Of A Leader* (Colorado Springs, CO: NavPress, 1988), 66.

18. Ibid,. 70

19. John 5; 19, 30; John 6:38; 8:26, 29, 38; 12:49

20. David Wiersbe and Warren W. Wiersbe, *Making Sense Of The Ministry* (Chicago, IL: Moody, 1983), *32.*

Chapter Nine – Twisted or Transformed?

1. Oswald Chambers, *The Psychology of Redemption* (London: Simpkin Marshall, 1947), 26-27.

2. Dallas Willard, *The Great Omission* (San Francisco, CA: Harper Collins Publishers, 2006), 61.

3. Ephesians 4: 17 – 31: Romans 6: 1 – 14; Colossians 3: 1 – 25; Romans 12: 1 – 21

4. Todd Hunter, *Giving Church Another Chance* (Downers Grove, IL: InterVarsity Press, 2010), 159.

5. Dallas Willard, *The Spirit Of The Disciplines* (San Francisco, CA: HarperCollins, 1988), 71.

6. Malcolm Gladwell (http://www.bottomlineperformance.com/10000-hours-to-mastery-the-gladwell-effect-on-learning-design/)

7. Eugene Peterson, *A Long Obedience In The Same Direction* (Downers Grove, IL: InterVarsity Press, 1980), 11-12.

8. Ethan Rouen, "Taking It To The Limit." *American Airlines Magazine*, May, 15, 2013.

9. Ivana Kottasova, "First Woman To Cross Antarctic Solo: I've never felt so alone." CNN, October, 5, 2012.

Chapter Ten – True Confessions Of Today's Christian Church

1. Dr. Richard J. Kredcir, "Statistics and Reasons For Decline." *Francis A. Schaeffer Institute of Church*

Leadership Development (2007). www.truespirituality.org

2. Richard Stearns, "Goodbye, Christian America; Hello True Christianity." *Hoff Post Review,* November, 11, 2012.

3. Shelley Shattuck, "7 Startling Facts: An Up Close Look at Church Attendance in America." *Church Leaders,* 2014. www.churchleaders.com

4. Todd D. Hunter, *Christianity Beyond Belief* (Downers Grove, IL: InterVarsity Press, 2009), 9.

5. Dr. Gordon L. Anderson, "Lecture: Lessons I've Learned From Forty-Five Years of Leading 17 November. 2014

6. Robert E. Quinn, *Deep Change* (San Francisco, CA: Jossey-Bass, 1996), 52.

7. Phyllis Tickle, "The Great Emergence: How Christianity is Changing and Why," review by Chuck Warnock, 26, September. 2008

8. Chuck Colson, *The Body* (Dallas, TX: Word Publishing, 1992), 30.

9. Ed Hays, *The Church* (Nashville, TN: Word Publishing, 1991), 54.

11. Donald G. Bloesch, *A Theology Of Word and Spirit* (Downers Grove, IL: InterVarsity, 1992), 272.

12. Dr. Henry and Richard Blackaby, *Spiritual Leadership* (Nashville, TN: B&H Publishers, 2001), 20.

13. David Watson, *Called And Committed* (Wheaton, IL: Harold Shaw Publishers, 1982), 36.

14. Ed Hays, *The Church* (Nashville, TN: Word Publishing, 1991), xii.

Chapter Eleven – The Church: Finding Our Focus

1. Dallas Willard, *Renovation of the Heart* (Colorado Springs, CO: NavPress, 2002), 235.
2. Dallas Willard, *The Great Omission* (San Francisco, CA: Harper Collins Publishers, 2006), 14.
3. A. W. Tozer, *I Call It Heresy* (Harrisburg, PN: Christian Publications, 1974), 5.
4. Dietrich Bonhoeffer, *The Cost of Discipleship* (New York, NY: Macmillan Publishing Co., 1963), 47.
5. Alan Hirsch, *The Forgotten Ways* (Grand Rapids, MI: Brazo Press, 2007), p102.
6. David Watson, *Called and Committed* (Wheaton, IL: Harold Shaw Publishers, 1982), 21.
7. Chuck Colson, *Loving God* (Grand Rapids, MI: Zondervan Publishing, 1983), 176.
8. Francis Schaeffer, From a lecture I heard from him many years ago.

PERSONAL NOTES

ABOUT THE AUTHOR

Ken is a pastor, speaker, author, and coach. His focus is to help Christians build and live a life that counts, and help Christian leaders live better and lead better.

OTHER RESOURCES

Ken's first book, *Unexpected: Navigating Life's Unforeseen Turns* is about Ken's late wife's passing and how he navigated through that very difficult season of life. But it's a book that's also written to help anyone navigate through their own times of difficulty and adversity.

COACHING

Ken offers three coaching tracks:
- For individuals - Eternal Impact: A 5 Step Strategy For Building And Living A Life That Counts
- For Christian Leaders - Staying Power: 5 Core Ideas To Sustainability In Christian Leadership
- For Writers - 6 Proven Steps For Writing A Good Book

PODCAST

Ken also has a monthly podcast for pastors and Christian leaders called *Live Better, Lead Better.*

To order Ken's book or for further information on any of these resources, visit Ken's personal website at www.kenlroberts.com

STAYING POWER

5 CORE IDEAS TO SUSTAINABILITY IN CHRISTIAN LEADERSHIP

KEN L ROBERTS

To order more copies of
Staying Power, paperback or eBook, or bulk orders –
go to www.kenlroberts.com